ONE MAN'S TRASH

A History of the Cigar Box Guitar

William J. Jehle

ONE MAN'S TRASH

ISBN 1453802398
EAN-13 9781453802397

To Ralph Jehle
My best role model because he thought he wasn't

Contents

Acknowledgments

It's one thing to tell yourself that you are going to write a book. It's quite another to actually sit down and do it. Through my career as a guitar player, recording artist, producer, guitar maker, marketer, salesman, and so on, I've always been capable of managing things myself. When my attention was consumed by the cigar box guitar, its origins, and its evolution, I found myself surrounded by helpful and encouraging people, without whom this work would not have been possible.

To Max Shores, producer of the "Songs Inside The Box" cigar box guitar documentary; somehow you managed to whittle down my 45 minute answer to your question about the cigar box guitar history into a neat 30 seconds. I spent months in preparation for your questions and what wound up on the cutting room floor became the impetus for this book. It was through my self-study and rumination in preparation for my interview with you that much of the material for this book was collected.

To Jim Fracassa for turning me on to cigar box guitars in the first place by pointing me to Make magazine, issue number 4, which included an article by Ed Vogel who built a cigar box guitar. Even though you derailed my plans to build an archtop guitar, and I will never build that guitar now, you started me on a course of discovery, revelation, and freedom from the staunch rules of crafting stringed instruments and I will never be able to look at their creation the same way again.

To Shane Speal, The King of the Cigar Box Guitar, original curator of the National Cigar Box Guitar Museum, and original historian and champion of the cigar box guitar, I owe a world of thanks. Once you were willing to part with the Cigar Box Guitar Museum and pass the honor of being curator to me, I've been privileged to examine the collection and add to it to produce the largest collection of cigar box instruments in the world. You provided me with a wealth of primary sources.

To John McNair, you have the keenest eye to pick out cigar boxes in dusty photographs and old newspapers. Your contribution to the timeline of events has been invaluable, even if you did make my work that much more difficult because I had to double my research efforts.

To Keni Lee Burgess, you provided exceedingly rare copies of cigar box fiddle plans. Rare finds like this are always a joy to discover, and they make me realize that even with years of digging and exploring through source material, there is always something else lurking out there left to be discovered.

To all the nameless and helpful librarians from the Library of Congress and from the small town local libraries I frequented over the past few years. Your patience with answering my questions and listening to me ramble on in encyclopedic dictations is kindly appreciated. Often, it was in those moments that new connections between disparate information were realized by your thoughtful suggestions.

To the writers I've talked to over the years, either in person or through the internet, you have been integral in giving me enough courage to make me think that I could achieve this work and see it through to publication. Deb DeSalvo, author of *The Language of the Blues*, contributor to *Rolling Stone*, and fellow Zen Guitarist, your publishing knowledge and encouragement have been invaluable to me as I struggled with the idea of writing anything at all. To Adrian Clark, columnist, musical editor, teacher, and recording artist for *Guitarist*, Future Publishing UK, and valuable friend, you have always been an inspiration as you never fail to see the humor in anything. To Bob Cianci, columnist for *Premier Guitar*, your wonderful article on cigar box guitars was a pleasure to see since it gave these humble instruments an air of the boutique. To Phil Sudo, who gave me the most important guitar lesson I ever had in *Zen Guitar*, this book follows your suggestion to share the experience. To David Sutton, remarkable photographer and gifted writer, you are a kindred spirit who picks up the history of the cigar box guitar where I leave off. We seem to be two sides of the same coin, you and me.

To my parents, you have been with me through my entire journey and exploration of all things guitar. I wouldn't be where I am today without your guidance, your willingness to put up with my constant craving to play guitars, and your reminders that I needed "a marketable skill and a safe car to drive." I have those covered now, so you did a good job. To my uncle Ralph Jehle, to whom I dedicate this work, despite the fact that you told me to find another role model, your humility and ability to work with your hands to create something wonderful constantly inspired me. The fact that you insisted that building "a Jehle guitar" was more than just putting someone else's work together and putting my name on it stung at the time. But without that, I may not have been so driven to carve guitars out of raw materials in quite the same way. I always wanted a beard like yours, too.

To Francesca Kazan's bookshelf on which sits works by people she knows, I acknowledge and apologize to the books on the left and right of this one. This little book will feel the better for being near those wise companions, if not a little taller.

William J. Jehle
September 2009

Foreword

"When I was younger I could remember anything, whether it had happened or not."

\- Mark Twain

To the average listener, music may be a passive experience. It walks with us through grocery stores and shopping malls, rides with us in our cars and elevators. While we meander through our day, music is there in the background. Occasionally, we may hear something and wonder who the artist is, or make a mental note that we want to add that song to our own collection. In these moments, we crave a repeated experience of reproducing that music at a later time. Recordings, being what they are, sound the same each time we hear them. It's a captured experience to release at any later time that we choose.

To me, music, guitar music in particular, has always been a mystery, a puzzle for me take apart and reassemble so that I could understand what made it work. As a guitarist, that was important because I not only wanted to reproduce the music that I heard, I wanted to recreate the music as an active experience. Later, as a guitar maker, to simply create the sounds was not enough. There was a feeling in each of the instruments that I held which was also part of the experience of performing music.

This great mystery of all things guitar began for me at an early age when I was around 5 years old. I credit a single event to the fact that I am the guitarist that I am today. I saw a performance of Roy Clark on television. He was playing "Under the Double Eagle," his signature song to this day, and where disaster could have struck, the most amazing thing I had ever seen happened. A single string on the guitar broke. It didn't even faze him because he kept on playing with the remaining five strings. A few seconds later, another string broke, leaving him with four strings. At this point he did stop playing and motioned for the band to stop playing as well. He said into the microphone, vocalizing what the audience, including me, was thinking at that point, "He's pickin' the strings right off of that thing!" And then it happened – he started playing the song again with the remaining 4 strings. The band joined in spurring him on, faster and faster. He never missed a note.

Even at such a young age, I was struck with two thoughts. First, since Clark broke those strings while he was playing, he *must* have needed them to play that song. Yet, he broke two strings in a row and managed to keep playing. How could this be? The guitar at that moment became a puzzle for me to figure out. I wanted to know how to play a song on a guitar like that. Despite the loss of strings, which were apparently optional now in the hands of the right player, the song could still be played. Secondly, I thought, no, I *knew* that I had to figure this puzzle out. I spun around to my mother and said, "I want to do *that*."

Given my age at the time, I lacked the ability to really say what *that* was. To my mom, it was a simple statement of "I want to play the guitar." That was just the beginning. What I really meant by *that* was that I wanted to unravel this mystery of how it was all connected, of how a guitar with its matrix of frets and strings could function while being broken. I can articulate this now without difficulty; all I knew at the time was that this was something I knew I needed to be a part of.

Unlike most of the musicians I studied in preparation for this book, I didn't cobble together a makeshift guitar out of found objects to get started. Perhaps I should have. I waited and persisted in telling my parents that I really wanted to have a guitar. By the time I was around 10 years old, my father and I went to a local music shop in town and he essentially let me have my pick. To my knowledge, I had never been given an opportunity like that before. It made my choice that much harder. Not knowing how to play a guitar didn't seem to be a big problem for picking one out though. I probably held and strummed each one, just fascinated enough with the fact that they sounded so nice and that I *made* that sound. Eventually I narrowed the choice down to two classical guitars. I remember that they both sounded nice, one slightly warmer and more mellow sounding than the other. I really wanted that one, but there was the second guitar that was pretty good. The only thing I remember about the second one is that it was cheaper than the one I really wanted. Somehow I managed to work up enough courage to ask my father for the more expensive one. There was probably an obligatory fatherhood question of, "are you sure that *this* is the one you want?" to which I answered or just nodded, "yes."

We drove home with that cherished guitar in the back of the family station wagon. I had no clue how to play it, so I would just look at it and brush my hands across the strings to hear that lovely tone. I thought to myself that I was *finally* going to figure this puzzle out. I had a *real* guitar.

Within a year or two, some new neighbors moved in next door. They had two sons, the oldest of whom also played guitar. I quickly got to know him. He played electric guitars though. I had never played an electric guitar before, so the feel of metal strings was strange to my fingers. Likewise, he was unfamiliar with classical guitar technique and some of the finger positions I played looked strange to him. At some point, he handed a pillow case with most of the parts to a Teisco Tulip in it to me. He said that someone else gave it to him like that and he had no use for it. It was mine for the taking if I wanted it.

Over the next several weeks I put that Teisco Tulip back together. I was no stranger to electronics by that time, and my dad had plenty of tools and the soldering iron that I needed to get it reassembled. I got a few parts and switches from the local Radio Shack to complete the circuitry. My uncle Ralph had a workshop in the back of his house and a piece of Formica scrap that he let me use to make a pickguard from. That was the first guitar that I built, or repaired. It wasn't a great guitar by any standard but I was proud of it because I made it work. Another part of the mystery of the guitar had been exposed then because I knew how to take one apart and put it back together again. I didn't realize it at the time, but the way in which I cobbled that first electric guitar together would become an integral part of my career as a guitar player and maker later in life. The joy of producing tone by finger pressure on strings was enhanced by the experience of knowing it was my hands in and on the instrument during its assembly and construction.

As the years went by, the guitar was my constant companion. It would console me when I was down, take my abuses when I was angry, and frustrate me as I tried to learn a new song. I remember feeling almost a sense of disappointment when I would eventually discover how to play certain songs correctly. They were no longer mysterious and I enjoyed them less when I heard them again. That particular puzzle had already been solved. I didn't need to hear it anymore.

To write a song on guitar, however, presented a different sort of challenge. There was no real mystery to creating music, since it seemed to flow automatically from my mind directly to my hands. Most of my playing was mechanical in those days, as I simply played whatever popped into my mind. However, occasionally one of those magical moments, those "happy accidents," happened when I would make a mistake in fingering or in picking something that was familiar. When those accidents happened, the mystery reappeared – my interest would be piqued again because some sound that I made needed to be investigated. In those moments, my expectations didn't connect to the sounds I heard. Not only did I want to know what I did wrong, I wanted to know how I could repeat it. I learned a lot from making those mistakes.

When I committed my songs to record, eventually starting my own label to sell them, I had many more accidents and moments of discovery to stay interested. To create a good sounding recording was yet another mystery to solve. I eventually discovered the art of layering guitars to create a rich sound. The problem, I would eventually come to find out, is that my guitars were all, in some way, flawed and noisy. Remembering my experience with my uncle Ralph many years earlier, I set out to create a single guitar that combined the best attributes of all my guitars and one that would record well. Ironically, it would be my quest for creating a single perfect guitar that would lead me to appreciate the idiosyncrasies and imperfections of every other guitar I played, particularly cigar box guitars. Before that revelation happened, I had to discover something else first.

As my small record label was going, the music I created didn't capture the attention of many people. The way I made guitars, however, did. For my fifth CD release, I created an experience that started with raw materials, followed through with the construction of a few electric guitars, and ended with an EP of songs that I performed on those guitars. For all the years that I explored the guitar as something to be deconstructed and personally explored, I realized that there were other people like me in the world that were eager to learn the same thing. Knowing that, I was ready to start my next project, a DVD that focused solely on building that perfect guitar. Not only would I continue to demystify the guitar for myself, I would share the experience with other potential guitar makers. Through that shared experience, I hoped to echo my own movement from producing a sound from hands on strings to creating a unique, personal, sound from the hands constructing an instrument. At least, that was my initial goal.

As I was writing and revising the script for the DVD, I received a message from a friend of mine. The message was simple; it was a link to an article on building a cigar box guitar with the added temptation of, "you have to check this out." After reading the article, I had a revelation – a true epiphany. To build a cigar box guitar was the ideal way to really demystify the construction of a guitar. Having made several traditional guitars before this time, and having worked with other new guitar makers, I realized we all had something in common. We all seemed to be over ambitious to create what we thought at the time was a *perfect* guitar. We would invest in tools, exotic tone woods, and, often, pay the price for making a mistake on our first efforts. The cigar box guitar was the antithesis of all of this. Cigar box guitars were cheap, simple to make, and most importantly, they didn't have this ideal set of measurements and materials to interfere with the creation of an instrument. That was the information that deserved to be covered in my DVD project. In the guitar makers' quest for perfection, we were overlooking the most basic and primal of musical instruments.

Within a couple of months, my DVD on *"How to Build a Guitar: The String, Stick, Box Method"* was complete. After its release, I discovered many other cigar box guitar makers in the world. Not only had I tapped into an idea rich with possibilities for beginners just getting started in making traditional guitars, I discovered an entire sub-culture already in existence dedicated to the cigar box guitar and its relatives.

Fueled with a curiosity about cigar box guitars from that point on, I started searching for everything I could to learn more about them. That search became an obsession to find a single source, a compendium on the history of cigar box guitars. While a handful of works stood out as being very good on a particular aspect, none of them really walked through the answers to when, and how, and why these instruments were created. More often than not, I would find a single mention of a musician who started out on a cigar box guitar, followed by their graduation to a traditional version of the instrument and the rest of the material would continue through their entire career – never again mentioning their humble beginning on a cigar box guitar. Was there not more than a single sentence or paragraph about those cigar box guitars these musicians started with? Could their instruments possibly still exist? Could I interview the players or their surviving family members to learn more? I wanted to know.

Thus, consider this book as a collection of parts to the history of cigar box guitar puzzle – its origins, and its changes in value and perception from the mid-1800s to the present. While I cannot promise that all the pieces are here, together we will assemble the disparate parts – snippets, one-line mentions, newspaper and magazine articles – into a cohesive whole. Where parts are missing, I have searched for substitutions or parallel events to fill in the gaps. It is my wish that through this process, other guitar players and makers will grow through the experience of producing sounds with their fingers on strings, to working with their hands on the instruments they play.

Introduction

"People write books they can't find on library shelves"
— George Orwell

As I began writing about the history of the cigar box guitar, there was not a word to describe such a narrow topic as the study of the cigar box guitar. During my research I began to see connections to many other fields of study, some of which on the surface seemed completely unrelated. I seemed to uncover a topic that was woven out of threads of human experience, human desires, as well as long threads on the ancestry of stringed instruments from European and from African traditions. The longer the thread, the more likely it was to tangle.

Detritomusicology

As the various threads were woven together I eventually coined my own term to describe my efforts, *detritomusicology*, from the root words *detritus* and *musicology*. While detritus may just be a fancy word for trash, it actually carries a connotation of organic waste that becomes the food stuffs for other matter. Detritus is meant to be and can be reused. Musicology is the study of music. Thus, *detritomusicology* is defined as the study of music made from discarded and reused material.

I suppose that giving a field of study a name is superfluous. However, under the umbrella of this term I have been able to broaden my study beyond the cigar box guitar. That is, I was free to investigate similar instruments, even those that predate the advent of the cigar box in the 1800s, the mindset of the player and builder of such instruments, or the social and financial aspects of popular culture and its influence on cigar box instrument makers. In short, it set up a meaningful boundary in which the cigar box guitar, cigar box violin, cigar box banjo, cigar box ukulele, and similar variants of the instrument could be contained. On the other hand, it also creates a problem for the study of a cigar box guitar. What is a guitar?

Consulting the Concise Oxford English Dictionary, a guitar is defined as a "six-stringed lute played with hand with fretted finger-board," to which I take several exceptions. First of all, guitars do not always have 6 strings. A tenor guitar, for instance, has only 4. Guitars played by modern guitarists can have 7 or 8 strings to extend their tonal range. Guitars which have pairs of strings, or courses, can have 10 to 12. Guitars can have multiple necks which increase the number of strings again and again. The second problem with the definition is that it defines a guitar as another instrument – a lute. True, the term *luthier*, roughly translated as "lute maker," does derive from the French *luth* for lute, and traditionally a luthier is an instrument maker of both plucked and bowed instruments, fretted and fretless instruments. I can almost accept the definition of a guitar as a form of lute based on that tradition. For similar reasons, I can almost accept the inclusion of a "fretted finger-board" in the definition of a guitar, but to that, I must also take exception.

What about the guitar's relatives in the banjo, ukulele, and mandolin? Their definitions are not much better. According to the Concise OED, the banjo is described as being a guitar neck with a tambourine body. The ukulele is described as a small Hawaiian four-string guitar. Both of those definitions point back to the guitar which, again, points back to the lute. The definition of mandolin departs from the Concise OED's propensity to define everything as a guitar, and retreats to describing the instrument as a member of the lute family with pairs of strings. It's all too specific, and much more exclusive than inclusive. These *guitars* or *lutes* made with cigar boxes don't follow such rules, even some of the more straight-forwarded rules as string count or that they are played "with hand." There are several examples of one-string cigar box guitars that are played with bottles or knife edges as a slide, and the notes are sounded by striking the string with a stick.

From a detritomusicologist point of view, I needed the definition of a more general term. Searching again through the Concise OED, I found a more suitable word – *instrument*. An instrument, particularly a musical instrument, is defined as a, "contrivance for producing musical sounds by vibration of string [as in stringed instruments], or of a body of air in pipe [as in wind instruments]." This definition is ideal, wide open to interpretation, and for that reason I will tend to describe cigar box guitars and its related creations as cigar box instruments interchangeably throughout the rest of the book.

Armed with the proper words to describe what I am investigating both as a field of study and the objects within it, I can now address how I will present the history of the cigar box instrument. During my research, I collected a wide variety of sources, from works of fiction, to plans to build cigar box instruments, to reviews on unrelated products that used the idea of cigar box instruments as a metaphor. The challenge, then, given the bulk of the information, was how to interpret all this data. Through inspection of common topics in the archives I could organize this history in at least three different ways. I could organize the information into a chronological list of events and interpret the connection of those events. I could organize information into thematically interesting and connected events, irrespective of the time in which they occur. Or, I could just present the archives as they are without interpretation. To simply list the artifacts as they are without interpretation, however, does not suffice to probe the mystery of the guitar for me. I have to treat the artifacts as clues, but clues to what?

What Is History

As a chronological listing of events, information about the cigar box reused in the craft of making an instrument does have several distinct periods. For instance, there are periods that directly follow economic catastrophe. The popular music during those financially difficult times is reflected in the type of instrument produced. There are noticeable eras that favor a violin, then a banjo, then a ukulele, and then ultimately a guitar. But then there are periods where the instrument is marginalized as a child's toy – something viewed as substandard and disposable.

Thematically linking events is suitable for examining their commonality and exploring interesting patterns, such as why particular people made cigar box instruments, the fact that they could be created by adults for something to make music with or that they could be made by children to learn to play music or to play (in the sense of not making real music, but pretending to be a musician). To interpret events through the course of the history in this way, the legitimacy of cigar box instruments became my primary interest.

Considering the age and circumstances of cigar box instrument players, early examples demonstrate adults' serious use of the instrument in the mid to late 1800s. By the late 1800s, the cigar box instrument became the focus as a child's first instrument, a theme which reached its peak in the 1920s. By the 1930s, cigar box guitars became just a brief step in the early path of many blues musicians. Typically, it is this type of musician that people associate with cigar box instruments. While it is likely and plausible that financial hardships were motivators for many blues musicians to create cigar box instruments, it is not always the case.

Looking at most of the evidence, cigar box instruments have been used by children as a substitute for a proper instrument, a tool to learn on and play with until a traditional version of the instrument could be made available, and also as toys to extend their own creative worlds. However, the evidence is also mixed with cigar box instrument use by adults as vehicles or gimmicks for purposes of entertainment, as substitutes for proper instruments where financial means, imprisonment, or warfare were blocking forces to getting a "real" instrument. Creative means to produce a musical instrument in these circumstances were necessary. However, even under such conditions, are cigar box instruments not "real?" They are not traditional or mass produced, but does that make them less legitimate? A typical rebuttal is that cigar box instruments are just not "traditional" but I have obvious problems with that statement. Plainly stated, how can so many hand-made instruments created from discarded materials like the cigar box, created in such various environments as the parlor, the back alley, or other conditions *not* be viewed as a tradition in and of itself? There is an even larger question, however: under what conditions is a cigar box instrument just a toy and when does it transition into a legitimate instrument? Is it possible that a cigar box instrument is something more than just an old re-used box?

How the Book Is Organized

This book is divided into five sections. The first two sections are interwoven. In other words, the first section presents chapters devoted to what I consider the most significant representative for a particular type of cigar box instrument, starting with cigar box violin, followed by the cigar box banjo, the cigar box ukulele, and the cigar box guitar. After examining these representatives of the cigar box instruments, the third section presents a timeline of events for that type of cigar box instrument, mostly in its entirety. Certain key points have been extracted to create the fourth section which groups cigar box instruments by theme, such as trench art during times of war, as children's toys or educational devices, or their most familiar form as a makeshift guitar for young musicians that went on to successful careers making music. The fifth and final section contains excerpts from the timeline and the stories of cigar box instruments to form a collection of cigar box instrument plans. In the first two sections it's interesting to observe not only how cigar box instruments were produced and how they were perceived, but in this final section, the presentation of the plans undergoes a dramatic change; the plans are aimed at the same audience, but there is a noticeable evolution in the way the plans are written.

Some may find tedious the sections which present timelines of events, because here, some material is simply quoted in its entirety. My research taught me that I tend to dislike books which are just a collection of resource material, and it wasn't my intent to reproduce this sort of book. I wanted to share insight beyond the raw source material and it was a disappointment when a simple search of the internet could retrieve the same information that I was reading. However, in order to present the most comprehensive account possible, here I have to do a little of both. First I wanted to establish a complete account for how cigar box instruments have been used, recalled by listeners, and portrayed in the media. In essence, I wanted to compile a complete collection of the source materials that I have been able to locate up to this time. Often these source materials consisted of a single line from much larger works. Secondly, I wanted to explore the more prominent people in the history of these instruments and to probe the unexpected and often surprising connections between them.

As far as the reference material is concerned for the content of this book, I have limited myself to artifacts which date from the year 2000 or before, with a single exception of an artifact which marks the 125th anniversary of the ukulele which dates from 2004. My decision to not pursue events beyond the year 2000 is simple: it's not history yet. The resurgence in interest for cigar box guitars and related cigar box instruments has created so much new information, many new cigar box instrument makers, recordings, interviews in magazines and newspapers, on television and radio programs that it would be far too arduous a task to collect all of that information in this book, and as this is a book of history, limiting my study to pre-2000 material was a necessary though not easy decision.

The Cigar Box

"If necessity is the mother of invention, discontent is the father of progress"
– David Rockefeller

I have noticed something curious about myself when I visit a museum. I have this internal drive and curiosity to find the oldest artifact therein – be it a coin, painting, weapon, or sculpture. Age alone, while fascinating, is not quite as exciting to the experience of seeing the first example of larger body of work, or of an entire movement in the art world: Works such as Monet's *Impression, Soliel Levant*, for which the Impressionist movement was named, or Alexander Calder's kinetic art from 1931 that would eventually become known as the common 'mobile,' hold a greater interest for me. As I explore deeper and deeper into the collections and displays in museums, I inevitably discover things that are older and closer to genesis artifacts. What I find so troubling about these small discoveries is that the moment I find something that slightly predates an earlier discovery, the example that I so greatly admired moments ago is suddenly forgotten. And, in my continued exploration, I overlook equally fascinating displays, and even cheapen their value as I think to myself, "It's not *that* old. I've seen something *much* older than that." It's perhaps an odd way of thinking about museum artifacts, but I am guilty of it.

So, too, I have been guilty of searching for the earliest and oldest examples of cigar box instruments. In my quest for finding the first evidence of cigar boxes reused as musical instruments, and their specific types in the form of violin, banjo, guitar, ukulele, mandolin, or something else unique, I neglected to appreciate the humble, garden variety, run-of-the-mill examples I found during my search.

Knowing that I will never be able to truly point to a single artifact as the first, or the oldest cigar box instrument because there is always something else lurking for me to find, I have to remind myself that the cigar box is just a piece of puzzle.

When the small cigar box was introduced into American culture it is important to note that the box itself was an invention as a form of packaging. Before the box, the most common form of packaging would have been in the form of barrels, sacks, and bags for bulk goods or foil wrappers for smaller items. Box making was its own craft as far back as the late-eighteenth and early-nineteenth centuries. According to Thomas Hine in *The Total Package*, the customers for those boxes included jewelers, pill sellers, and others who sold low-bulk, high-value goods. As the technology for box-making improved, the folding paperboard box could be folded at the time of sale. While this solved the problem of empty setup boxes taking up as much room as full ones for the storekeeper, it added the burden of actually folding the box around a form at the time of sale – the exact same technique used by the box makers before.

The Cigar Box

For the cigar box as an invention, there was not a genesis event (with one possible exception that I will get to in a moment) that suddenly released the cigar box as we know it today into the world as a commodity object. Through innovation, the size, shape, and composition of cigars boxes changed over a period of decades.

Tony Hyman, curator for the National Cigar Museum, shares the background for the cigar box in his seminal work, *Handbook of Cigar Boxes*. Hyman notes that for the export trade, sturdy packaging in the form of a barrel which held 5,000 cigars was common during the early 1800s. By the mid 1800s shopkeepers demanded smaller packages, so the practice of wholesalers breaking down the barrel-sized lots and repacking them into purchased, empty cigar boxes came into practice. Due to the Federal Revenue Act passed in 1865, it was required that cigars be packed in boxes before they could leave the factory. Cigar factories started to manufacture their own boxes as a result. And, as the demand for cigars increased in the 1880s, box companies proliferated to meet the increasing demand for boxes. During the 1870s and 1880s, an IRS law that required cigars to be packed in wooden boxes was revised to include other materials including pasteboard, paper, enameled tin, or other metal boxes approved as substitutes for wooden boxes, and later revised again to include glass jars and plastic. One of the earliest surviving cardboard cigar boxes from an unknown box maker dates to the 1880s. The design was ahead of its time because a nearly identical design didn't appear again until the 1900s. By the 1920s and 1930s, most cigar boxes were made of cardboard. Cardboard was first used as a substitute for wood for box lids, then the lids and bottoms. By the late 1940s and early 1950s, the all-cardboard box became popular throughout the cigar and cigar box industries.

Wooden boxes, however, continue to be produced for their aesthetic of quality, and because certain woods are favored for storing and aging cigars.

The closest thing to a genesis event for the invention of the cigar box as an invention per se happened between 1863 to 1865. First, according to Hyman's handbook of cigar boxes, as the Civil War was nearing its end, in 1863 the sale of cigars in boxes of 1,000 was made illegal. Second, it would take another two years for the Federal Revenue Act to pass into law the regulation that the number of cigars in a box were restricted to 25, 50, 100, 250, and 500. The numbers of cigars in boxes had a practical application in that only five denominations of revenue stamps would need to be printed. Primarily, these two government regulations which limited the numbers of boxed cigars affected the size and shape of the box – important because it somewhat presciently restricted the cigar box to a size suitable for reuse in stringed instruments.

Before 1863 cigar boxes could be any size, and it is both possible and likely that a few were of a similar size and shape to what they are today as evidenced by two early advertisements located in Tony Hyman's National Cigar Museum.

1789

According to Tony Hyman, consumer size boxes of 100 cigars were offered for sale in a 1789 New York City newspaper. This is the earliest confirmed mention of a box of 100 cigars found at the time of this writing. Typically, cigars (also sometimes called "segars") during this time were sold in boxes (1,000), half-boxes (500), or quarter-boxes (250).

1811

Hyman observes that ads for consumer-size boxes of 100 cigars appeared in an advertisement in an unidentified Philadelphia based newspaper:

> Tobacconist Andrew Mitchell "respectfully informs the Public that he has constantly for sale, at the most moderate prices, Spanish Segars, of a superior quality, manufactured by himself, and warranted to be made of the first quality of Cuba tobacco, in boxes containing 100 to 1000 segars."

Reuse

Size, shape, and composition aside, cigar boxes all shared the same attribute. They could not be reused to sell goods again once the tax seal was broken. Since cigar boxes were mostly made of wood, they would likely earn a place as fuel for burning to warm the house or heat the stove. A few survived to store scraps of paper or sewing items such as "odd pieces of tape and strings" or a "box for old buttons" as Lydia Maria Child instructed in *The American Frugal Housewife* in 1829. A few more survived and were repurposed as the raw materials to create something else such as gifts and toys as expertly shown in Albert Neely Hall's 1911 work *Handicraft for Handy Boys*. Hall's book included plans for several wagons, pieces of doll-house furniture, a rather spooky looking jack-in-the-box using a decapitated doll's head on a spring, and less traumatic handy items like a dust broom holder, small clock shelf, match box for the kitchen, and letter holder, all made from the wood of cigar boxes.

Cigar boxes, while a great source for scrap wood for projects including stringed instruments, were not the sole source of materials. As Paul Oliver noted in *Savannah Syncopators: African Retentions in the Blues,*

> It does not seem unlikely that the custom of making a fiddle, guitar or banjo from available materials – lard can, broomhandle, fence picket, cigar box, or whatever may be at hand that meets the ingenuity of the maker – has a history that extends back to the enslavement and beyond.

While searching through archives for what I was determined to find as the first cigar box instrument, I collected a number of one-line mentions of other detritus based instruments. This list is not intended to be exhaustive but is provided as more of a demonstration of the culture of creating musical instruments from scrap materials. Here are a few of my favorite examples.

1777

From Denison Olmsted's Memoir of Eli Whitney, Esq., we learn of a remarkable young Eli Whitney, born December 8, 1765, who makes his first violin around age 12. Though it predates the cigar box as we know it today, and the materials used by Whitney are unknown, it is relevant for the inventiveness of a youth to create music and finding the means to create an instrument.

The Cigar Box

At an early age, according to the memoir, Eli had a passion for mechanical things. From his father's workshop, Eli would make wheels and chairs with the variety of tools and his father's lathe. Sometime after Eli's mother had passed away, his father was away from home for a couple of days which left Eli full advantage of his father's workshop. When Eli's father returned, he asked the housekeeper about what Eli had been doing. The memoir states:

> 'She replied, 'he has been making a fiddle.' He was at this time about twelve years old [ca. 1777]. His sister adds that this fiddle was finished throughout, like a common violin, and made tolerably good music. It was examined by many persons, and all pronounced it to be a remarkable piece of work for such a boy to perform. From this time he was employed to repair violins, and had many nice jobs, which were always executed to the entire satisfaction, and often to the astonishment, of his customers.

1853

In this early example we learn about Theodore, a character appearing in "Walks Up Hill" by H. Spicer Esq., published in *New Monthly Magazine* with the mention that "he played the guitar and violin (the latter of which made by himself from the remains of an old tea-chest)."

> Theodore was an indefatigable talker; the life and soul of the couriers' room; holding his associates there, at the same time, in a sort of brotherly contempt that rather increased than diminished his popularity. He was a genius of the most

versatile character. He cooked, he sang, he played the guitar and violin (the latter instrument made by himself from the remains on an old tea-chest); he spoke every language under the sun – and more, for he had words that certainly belonged to none, including patois, which generally resembles its original tongue as much as Coptic. He was accomplished in the lighter arts of shooting, fishing, billiards, and skittles; and, lastly, told excellent stories, which latter, if the did occasionally borrow a tint or so from his fervid German imagination, were at least innocent of any deception – the little deviations from rigid truth being of the most lucid and transparent kind.

Theodore, while likely fictional, was depicted as well educated, charismatic - a real renaissance man. I am encouraged by Theodore and the fact that he made his own violin from a tea chest. Cigar box instruments fashioned out of available materials are often dismissed as a necessity due to poverty, but that ignores and undervalues the fundamental motivation to make an instrument in the first place. Musicians are, after all, creative people. Spicer's description of Theodore is similar to young Eli Whitney where motivation to create such a contraption was more about discovery and creative expression than overcoming financial deficiency.

1856

Published in *The Geneva Express*, May 3, 1856, Volume 1, Number 31, is a brief description of the Aeolian harp and a description on how one can make an Aeolian harp of their own. Given the description of its construction, it would not be difficult to create an Aeolian harp from a cigar box.

THE AEOLIAN HARP

There are few musical instruments, even when managed with the skill of a master, which produces a melody more delicate and enchanting to unsophisticated ears than the Aeolian harp. Its tones are wild and irregular; but plaintive and harmonious, resembling the wild bursts of unearthly music so often described in the pages of oriental romance as the music of the spheres. It is singular that these simple instruments are not oftener seen in the dwelling houses of our people. They "discourse most excellent music," without taxing the time or the purse of any individual. Placed in the window of a hall or chamber during the spring or summer months, the gentle breeze will play a tune upon them which cannot be imitated by human hands.

The construction of this instrument is simple, as the Aeolian harp is nothing more than a rectangular box made of thin pieces of pine wood. Its length may be equal to to [sic] the width of the window in which it is intended to be placed, and should be about five inches deep and eight inches wide. The upper surface of the box should be pierced with sounding holes, similar to those in a violin. Over this surface is stretched several strings, which require to be regularly tuned. Where the instrument is exposed to the action of a brisk breeze, it will sound forth the most agreeable combination of musical tones changing according to the ever varying impulses of the wind. The harp may be of any size, and the tones will correspond to the magnitude of the instrument.

ca. 1840

The earliest evidence of a cigar box instrument in the form of a violin is credited to Bostonian Charles A. White, an African-American composer, who according to legend, is thought to have made a cigar box violin "at an early age." As David Ewen notes in *Popular American Composers from Revolutionary Times to the Present*, White, in his boyhood, unable to purchase a violin, taught himself to play on the violin of his own making. Later in his career, White would be a lyricist, songwriter and publisher. White published his first song, *The Windows in the Cottage by the Sea-Side*, in 1868 and by 1870 became his own publisher with the hit *Come, Birdy, Come*. By 1884, White was notable, even as a minor composer, to have written the Democratic Party's *President Cleveland's Victory March*.

Given White's birth year of 1830, and reckoning that by "an early age" places him between the age of 10 and 19, an age consistent with other young cigar box violin makers, it places the first evidence of the cigar box violin very near the introduction of the cigar box as we recognize them today.

According to Tony Hyman, cigar boxes in their now familiar form didn't appear until around 1840. Setting that information alongside White's early cigar box violin, it is possible that the very first mention of a cigar box violin coincides with the familiar form of the cigar box in that same year. Even if White didn't make his cigar box violin until the end of his teens, however, it would still place the first evidence of a cigar box violin, at the latest, in 1849 – nearly a quarter century before Edwin Forbes's legendary copper etching of two Civil War soldiers playing a cigar box violin, which was published and copyright in 1876.

Edwin Forbes

"By stripping down an image to essential meaning, an artist can amplify that meaning..."
                        - Scott McCloud

After the trace evidence of the cigar box violin made by Charles A. White, the first significant evidence of a cigar box instrument in America actually starts in England in 1821 with the birth of Henry Carter. It would be Henry Carter's eventual career with the legendary P. T. Barnum, and later, Carter's tenacity for success as an illustrator that would lead to one of the most significant pieces of evidence for a cigar box violin to be captured by an American landscape painter named Edwin Forbes.

Who Is Henry Carter?

The question "who is Henry Carter?" is answered by J. G. Lewin in *Witness to the Civil War.*

Henry Carter was born in 1821 to a family well established in the glove-manufacturing business in Ipswich, Suffolk, England. It was assumed that

Henry, as the eldest son, would participate in the company, but he had other ideas. He favored wood carving and drawing, although his father disapproved.

In the family workshops Henry was exposed to silversmiths and their craft. He took an interest in their work and accumulated an impressive set of engraver's tools. At age seventeen Henry was sent to London to gain business experience in a wholesale dry-goods house. In the city, he pursued business training by day and drawing, in secret, by night. He began to submit sketches to various magazines, but fearing his father would object and call him home, he used for his submissions the pseudonym Frank Leslie. It worked. His sketches were accepted, and his father was none the wiser until Frank Leslie was well along with this new career.

By the age of twenty-two, Henry Carter was *London Illustrated*'s superintendent of engravers and was instrumental in the development of the new technique of "light-on-shade" line engraving. He made quite a name for himself, or more precisely, for Frank Leslie. Then, in 1848, he packed his tools and his pseudonym and immigrated to the United States, where he immediately legally changed his name to Frank Leslie.

Soon after Leslie's (né Carter) arrival in the States, he worked with P. T. Barnum as an illustrator between 1848 and 1849. According to Barnum's recollections in his work *Struggles and Triumphs*:

During the year 1848, Mr. Frank Leslie, since so widely known as the publisher of several illustrated journals, came to me with letters of introduction from London, and I employed him to get up for me an illustrated catalogue of my Museum. This he did in splendid manner, and hundreds of thousands of copies were sold and distributed far and near, thus adding greatly to the renown of the establishment

Several years later, in 1852, Leslie went to work with Barnum again in New York, where he became illustrator and chief engraver for Barnum's *Illustrated News*, which went out of business within a year. According to Barnum in his own writings, to say that his *Illustrated News* flopped would be to admit failure. Not so curiously, even a failure can be spun into gold by Barnum as he mentions in his *Autobiography*:

In the fall of 1852 a proposition was made by certain parties to commence the publication of an illustrated weekly newspaper in the city of New York. The field seemed to be open for such an enterprise and I invested twenty thousand dollars in the concern as special partner in connection with two other gentlemen who each contributed twenty thousand dollars as general partners. Within a month after the publication of the first number of the Illustrated News which was issued on the first day of January 1853 our weekly circulation had reached seventy thousand. Numerous and almost insurmountable difficulties for novices in the business continued however to arise and my partners becoming wearied and disheartened with constant over exertion were anxious to wind up the enterprise at the end of the first year. The engravings and good will of the concern were sold to the proprietor of Gleason's Pictorial in Boston who merged our subscription list with his. I came out of this enterprise without loss.

For Leslie, the experience with Barnum, however brief, was invaluable because he picked up a showman's trick or two, among them – sensationalism. Leslie had made the right business connections and set aside capital to start his own journal after Barnum's *Illustrated News* came to an end. J. G. Lewin continues with Leslie's success story:

> Encouraged by the success of [his first] two publications [Frank Leslie's Ladies Gazette of Fashion and Fancy Needle Work, and New York Journal], Leslie pressed on, and in 1855 Frank Leslie's Illustrated Newspaper appeared. Known as Leslie's Illustrated, this periodical combined Frank Leslie's talents as an illustrator with timely journalism and a good measure of Barnum-styled sensationalism. From the start, Leslie's Illustrated was a success with the reading public.
>
> Among the journals' innovations was the assembly-line method Leslie developed for illustration engraving. The traditional painstaking and time-consuming process of one engraver producing an entire image at once had been neither efficient nor profitable. Leslie changed that process. He divided the illustrating into sections, each two inches square, and assigned them to different engravers. When completed, the sections were assembled into a unified whole from printing. This reduced, from weeks to days, the time it took to prepare an illustration, and allowed for the swift publication of a newsworthy image.

[On the brink of bankruptcy], the lessons learned from Barnum soon came into play. The other major innovation of Frank Leslie's Newspaper was the introduction of sensationalism into journalism. The objective, after all, was not just to publish a newspaper, but to make a good profit by publishing a newspaper. Leslie achieved his objectives by sensationalizing the past week's incidents. Fires became conflagrations. Scuffles become brawls. Demonstrations become riots.

The circulation of Frank Leslie's Illustrated Newspaper was close to one hundred thousand in 1860, and by 1862, the second year of the war, it had more than doubled.

Special Artists of the Civil War

In 1862 Frank Leslie hired Edwin Forbes to join a corps of artists he was sending south to provide illustrations of the Civil War for his paper. As a pictorial reporter Forbes was known as "special correspondent" or "special artist." Armed with a pencil and a sketch pad, the twenty-three-year-old Forbes marched to war under the banner of *Frank Leslie's Illustrated Newspaper.*

Originally, Edwin Forbes was born in New York in 1839 with the name John Edwin Forbes. Early on he dropped "John" and from then on was known as simply Edwin Forbes. He began to study art in 1857 in classical fashion, painting animals, landscapes, and genre. With the outbreak of the Civil War in 1861 and working for Frank Leslie, Forbes's artistic career turned in a completely different direction.

Forbes, in the two-and-a-half years he covered the war, spent most of his time with the Army of the Potomac in Virginia, where he would remain until the autumn of 1864. During that time, according to William J. Cooper, Jr. in his introduction to *Thirty Years After*:

> Forbes had a straightforward mission – to sketch scenes of the war that would end up as illustrations in Frank Leslie's Illustrated Newspaper. He had to learn his craft quickly, for he had not previously done any commercial artwork. His artistic ability along with his energy and determination enabled him to become proficient rapidly. Like so many other new soldiers, Forbes discovered that battles were not exactly what he had imagined. He remarked that he had expected to accompany troops into battle and "seat myself complacently on a convenient hillside and sketch exciting incidents at my leisure." Forbes found that strategy to be impossible, however. At his first battle… he heard musket fire and wanted to watch the infantry charge. But he quickly learned that Confederate artillery raked the ridge which offered the best view of the fighting. In addition, Forbes admitted that the sight of wounded soldiers being moved toward the rear did not serve to drive him forward.

Perhaps as a result, Forbes concentrated on scenes he could witness close at hand – the everyday life of the soldiers their day-to-day movements. Leslie, his employer ever in the search for sensational battle scenes, liked the action coverage best, and because of that preference, fewer than half of Forbes's wartime sketches ended up being reproduced in *Frank Leslie's Illustrated*

Newspaper. For the sketches that did appear in the paper, Cooper describes the process as:

> The sketches drawn by Forbes had to undergo a transformation in New York City before they reached newspaper buyers. The engravers redrew every field sketch on wood, cut away the inked sections, and then made a metal impression. The skill of the engraver affected the fidelity with which the sketches were reproduced. In this instance Forbes was fortunate to work for Leslie, who, as a former engraver, understood the critical importance of the engraver's role better than anyone else in the business. He personally supervised the preparation of each illustration for his Illustrated Newspaper. Most of Forbes's sketches were faithfully copied by engravers, though they were sometimes adjusted in size or perspective to fit the layout of the paper.

> Leslie devised a system that greatly expedited the process of turning an artist's sketch into a newspaper illustration. Larger engravings required numerous blocks of wood, which were bolted together. For his large engravings Leslie had the blocks unbolted and the sections distributed to individual engravers to complete portions of the engraving. Then the blocks would be rebolted. In this way large engravings could be produced in almost the same time it took to complete one small engraving.

Evidence of this engraving technique are, upon close inspection of Forbes's etchings, duplicated in the 39 prints first published in book form in 1876 as *Life Studies of the Great Army.*

Home, Sweet Home

A scene in winter camp: Two soldiers sitting in front of their quarters, which are built with logs plastered with clay, and covered with canvas. The soldier sitting on the drum is playing the old tune on an improvised fiddle made from a cigar box, while the younger sits leaning against the mud chimney, which is crowned with a ploughshare to keep the smoke from blowing into the tent. (Text from a later edition of *A Civil War Artist at the Front*)

Upon close inspection of Forbes engraving of the two Civil War soldiers with the cigar box violin, evidence of the joining blocks can be seen. About every two inches in a grid, there is a line where the blocks met. These lines are cleverly hidden in a horizon, on the edge of a pair of pants, the edge of a building. But sometimes the line is in a clear area where no convenient place to hide the division is available. Even in the worst case, such visible lines are only a slight lightening of the ink. Casual observers may not even notice.

Sketchy Details

Knowing that an etching first had to be sketched before they were copied to wood blocks and cast onto metal plates, I became curious about the remains of any sketch from which Forbes's cigar box violin etching was copied. An arduous search led me to the Library of Congress where I found a collection of Forbes's sketches including those used for the 1876 edition of *Life Studies of the Great Army*. The first time I saw the drawing I was surprised to see that it was a mirror image with the single exception of the word "Figaros" brand on the cigar box.

> [When] Forbes departed the army and returned to New York City in the autumn of 1864, almost immediately upon his resettling in New York City Forbes reclaimed his original sketches from Leslie and began work on a project that would become his greatest artistic achievement. Between 1865 and 1868 he completed drawings of forty scenes based on his wartime sketches, which were then transferred to ground copper plates. In 1876 he exhibited the resulting etchings as *Life Studies of the Great Army*.

Having found the original sketch of "Home, Sweet Home," I wondered why Forbes waited nearly 11 years to release the sketches as etchings. Reading through William Forest Dawson's foreword to *A Civil War Artist at the Front*:

> From his on-the-spot drawings Forbes made a series of etchings, reproduced in a portfolio, first published without text in 1876. Originally entitled *Life Studies of the Great Army: A Historical Art Work*

in Copper Plate Etching Containing Forty Plates, the set of prints first sold for twenty-five dollars, later for fifty dollars, and signed impressions on India paper brought as much as three hundred dollars.

Home Sweet Home, in sketch form predates the lithograph

My speculation is that it was the cost of the paper that set the publication date at 1876. By the 1870s America was importing increasingly expensive rag fibers for paper from England, India, and China. Rags were in short supply in America which often resulted in people handing over used clothing as well as existing books to be recycled into paper. The demand for paper with a shortage of useable materials to make it drove the price higher. In the mid 1870s, however, the viable use of wood pulp to make paper made it very cheap to produce. America had ample trees to produce the wood pulp needed for paper. Susan Strasser in her book, *Waste and Want,* covers some of the pivotal moments in papermaking around this time.

With an ever-increasing demand for paper, and a worldwide rag shortage sent rag prices steadily upward decade after decade and inspired the search for rag substitutes... during the Civil War when cotton was scarce, the Associated Press promoted corn husks. Wood, straw, rope fibers including hemp, jute and esparto grass were also competitors.

Of all the possible rag substitutes, wood was the most promising, thanks to vast North American forests. The first successful process for grinding wood and converting it to pulp was developed in Germany, where commercial wood pulp paper production began in 1847. Eventually, an American group set up a company to produce wood pulp using German machines and methods. It shipped its first load of pulp to the Smith Paper Company in 1867.

Wood pulp paper was even less strong and durable than paper made from straw, but it was cheap. As it became widely available, newsprint prices dropped rapidly, from twenty-five cents a pound in the 1860s to two cents a pound in 1897. Most newspapers adopted the new stock in the late 1870s and early 1880s.

With wood pulp paper in use to print periodical newspapers and magazines, the demand for the higher rag content papers would be less and drop their price. Forbes could afford the slightly more expensive, but higher-quality India paper which was based on bleached hemp and rag fibers. The hemp content in the paper could not be completely bleached white, and as a result, tended to have a manila color. Dawson continues to describe the later releases of Forbes work:

In 1891, Forbes continued to derive his livelihood from work based on his wartime observations and experiences, and published a second volume of Civil War drawings, *Thirty Years After: An Artist's Story of the Great War Told and Illustrated with Nearly 300 Relief-etchings after Sketches in the Field and 20 Half-tone Equestrian Portraits from Original Oil Paintings*. For this collection, which was issued in 'twenty *divisions*' at fifty cents each or bound by '*sections*' in flexible English cloth at three dollars, he made about 220 additional etchings and wrote an informal text of reminiscences to accompany them.

Not too unlike India paper, English cloth was another high rag content paper made with materials imported from England. My speculation, again, is that this paper was chosen for its superior qualities for artworks and not for its price since wood pulp would have been a much cheaper alternative. Again, Strasser states:

> European rags cost more than American ones, but they offered manufacturers higher quality, especially Irish linen. By 1850, few Americans dressed in linen, a fabric still made by hand. Used for the best paper, it had to be imported from less industrialized countries. Unlike silk or wool, cotton and linen both offered high cellulose content, but linen was particularly strong because of its long fibers. Cotton rags could be supplemented with more expensive raw cotton, but premium paper contained at least one-third linen.

In Forbes's subsequent works, he added increasing bits of detail for each of the scenes he portrayed in his etchings. In 1890 Forbes produced *Thirty Years After: An Artist's Story of the Great War*. In it with his own words and pictures he recounts his experiences in the Great War. As Cooper describes Forbes expanding volume on the Civil War:

> Almost three hundred etchings taken from Forbes's field sketches, including those in *Life Studies of the Great Army*, dominate *Thirty Years After*.

> Forbes wanted his readers to understand what it meant to be a soldier in the Union army. For him the army was a living, breathing organism, whose inner workings he desired to reveal. He would accomplish this goal by illuminating almost every possible area of soldier life. To meet this end he divided *Thirty Years After* into eighty brief chapters, or more accurately snapshots, because the illustrations make up such a critical part of the book. They impart the essence of particular activities, whether feeding the troops or withstanding a charge.

> Forbes's soldiers spent much time tending to the same tasks that would occupy a civilian. Activities such as cooking, eating, washing, and leisure pursuits... including whiling away hours reading newspapers, playing cards, fishing, and even making and then playing a violin.

Home Sweet Home - Thirty Years After

Edwin Forbes added a great deal of detail for *Thirty Years After*. His recollection of details for the soldiers, their careful crafting of the cigar box violin, and the camaraderie among the soldiers while requesting a song is exceptional.

I was attracted on afternoon by strains of this sweet old melody, and as they touched the chord of memory so easily aroused in the desolation of army life, I strolled in direct of the plaintive sounds and came upon the scene my large picture portrays. I stood at a respectful distance till the air was finished, for it seemed like intrusion to come suddenly upon the two men whose thoughts I knew floated off to lonely Northern homes; but the notes soon ceased, and the violinist smiled a welcome as he laid down his instrument.

Stepping forward, I asked permission to examine the unique *Cremona*. The body was improvised from a cigar box, with the name "Figaro" burned in the wood. The neck was of soft pine, whittled into shape, and containing holes for the crude pine keys. The bridge and tail-piece were made of cedar, and the strings, which were of good quality, were obtained in Washington. The bow was skillfully made of pine wood and reddish-brown horse-hair.

Noticing the color, I said, "Where did you get this horse-hair?" The fellow remarked sheepishly, "From your mare's tail, when she was tied near here. I took it because it was so long." I assured him that no harm had been done and talked a bit with his companion, a drummer-boy. I found him to be a loquacious youth, like most of his craft, and also that he considered himself an authority on the beauties of music. I said I should like to hear the violin again, and the drummer suggested various tunes—some pathetic, some lively, and a number of military airs popular in camp, the performance of which he criticized quite professionally. "Home, Sweet Home" was repeated with amusing effect at pathos, but I had to admit that the tones were wonderfully good from so rude a little instrument.

Most of the soldiers' feelings found expression in music. Its influence both saddened and brightened their lives as they went from "grave to gay." Their life seemed to make them simple-hearted, and merriment gave a zest to existence while the shedding of pent-up tears many times alleviated sorrow—especially the soldier's greatest grief, home-sickness.

The soldiers' love of home was an ever-present memory. They universally kept up a regular correspondence with their families, and the mail at headquarters was equal to that of a fair-sized city. There was a regular system, each regiment, brigade and corps having a mail department, where letter were collected daily and promptly sent North. Those received from home were delivered without delay, troops often receive letters while lying under fire.

It was always a difficult matter to obtain a furlough; but when an application was granted, the soldier's spirits became most jubilant. Young as most of them were, right from the home fire-side, with not the remotest idea of the hardships to which they would be exposed, it is not to be wondered at that a visit to the old home was a great pleasure. I can see them now, with bright faces and spruce new uniforms, donned for the occasion, bidding good-by to comrades and hastening to the railroad depot. These visits were of great benefit, often restoring to health and spirits ill and dejected men. Received at home with jubilation and sent off again with honor an their return they would step briskly into the ranks and march forward to battle or to long and weary marches with cheerful courage.

Making a Cremona – tailpiece at the end of the text for "Home Sweet Home"

None but a soldier knows what the terrible army home-sickness was; how the men drooped and grew listless in the longing for home, and how many really died from the malady.

Thoughts of home came to the sick and wounded who were at time placed under trees or exposed to sun and rain, and their despondency often aggravated their condition. If a soldier was fortunate enough to get to a large general hospital in the rear, how his hard would beat with joy at the sigh of some relative, who had come on to wait upon him or if possible to take him home!

Ah yes, whether in the camp-fire's blaze, on the long march or in the crash of battle, the song of our soldiers most often heard was "Home, Sweet Home!"

Rebellion

Frank Leslie worked himself into an engraving career against his father's wishes and ultimately became a very successful illustrator, and, later, recognized as a pioneer in engraving. Frank Leslie was able to quickly turn sketches into reproducible images for his newspapers. Leslie's employee Edwin Forbes was driven away from the frontlines to escape possible death and injury to focus on safer subjects such as the soldiers at camp. As a result, Forbes got an opportunity to capture two soldiers playing a cigar box violin to pass the time and entertain themselves.

Edwin Forbes is only one many illustrators hired by Frank Leslie during the Civil War. Like Forbes, who was 23 years old when he started working as an illustrator for Leslie, most of the special artists were young men in their early 20s who were not sure of their life's work yet. The most prolific and best-known special artist at the time was English-born Alfred Waud. The special artist who went on to the greatest renown as a serious artist was Winslow Homer. Interestingly, among the lesser known special artists working under the banner of *Frank Leslie's Illustrated Newspaper* was a young man from Ohio, Frank Beard, whose younger brother Daniel was only 11 years old at the beginning of the Civil War – too young to enlist as a soldier or even as a drummer boy. Young Daniel Carter Beard would also eventually become an illustrator for Frank Leslie and for Mark Twain. But it's not his work with Leslie or Twain for which he is best known.

Perhaps Leslie's childhood rebellion would have been well received by Daniel Carter Beard. It was Beard's want for boys to escape from a stifled urban existence to regain a sense of being little savages again. It was as if Leslie's rebellion against his father and his family tradition, the Civil War rebellion between North and South, and the end of the Civil War with the emancipation of African-American slaves set the stage for Daniel Carter Beard to appropriate the banjo as a symbol of young boys return to being little savages and to lead their own rebellion against an increasingly stale urban existence.

Daniel Carter Beard

"I have tried to make my readers love nature, especially the primitive wilderness — unmanicured, unshaven, without a haircut."

-Daniel Carter Beard

When I first began learning about cigar box guitars, Daniel Carter Beard, after Edwin Forbes, is the next significant name in the history of these instruments. Two things in particular stand out about Beard. First, he was the founder of the Boy Scouts of America, and second, he was responsible for publishing the first known set of plans for a cigar box instrument – the Uncle Enos Banjo as Beard consistently called it.

The Boy Scouts of America
and Mark Twain

As I started investigating the origins of the Boy Scouts of America another name quickly came to surface, *also* as the founder of the Boy Scouts, Robert Baden-Powell,

who, incidentally, pioneered the use of hot-air balloons
in military spying. How could it be that both Beard and
Powell were attributed to be, apparently independently,
the founder of the Boy Scouts?

Quite by surprise Daniel Cater Beard answers this
question in his autobiography almost as if he anticipated
my question or had been asked this same question many
times before. He does little to question the origin of the
Boy Scouts or to claim to be their sole creator in his
autobiography.

> Undoubtedly Scouting came in part from different
> sources. Many people contributed effort and ideas
> to the movement. It was brought into being in the
> American way: by the efforts of a group of people.

> There are many who squabble about the origin of
> Scouting. They have lost sight of the forest
> through looking at the trees. The important fact is
> that Scouting now is a great, growing movement
> with a membership of more than a million
> youngsters [in 1936] in this country. These
> youngsters and the predecessors will be those who
> will preserve for future generations this great
> liberty-loving democracy that means so much to
> us.

> Here in the United States we, the descendants of a
> mighty set of hardy pioneers, now find ourselves
> in a new age – the "push-button" age. We no
> longer go to the well and drink from the old oaken
> bucket; we touch a button and a pitcher of ice
> water is brought to us. We no longer walk; we ride
> in luxurious machines. We no longer write our
> own speeches and reports; they are written for us
> and we sign them.

We must be on our guard to see the modern conditions do not soften our fiber until, when confronted with hardships, we become as helpless as a hermit crab without a shell.

In Beard's own words, his involvement with the Scouting movement overshadowed his other accomplishments: "My connection with the Boy Scouts of America seems to have wiped my past history off the slate." In my research, ironically, his involvement with Scouting only became obvious after I learned about his plans to build an Uncle Enos banjo; these plans remain easily available today in Beard's *The American Boy's Handy Book*.

With Beard so heavily credited with the Scout movement, it seems likely that *The American Boy's Handy Book* would have become the handbook for the Boy Scouts. Beard was asked to write such a handbook, but instead the work was compiled by Ernest Thompson Seton who, incidentally, was appointed as the first Chief Scout. Seton added romantic woodcraft and Indian lore to a British book already in existence for English Scouts.

Searching for the Uncle Enos Banjo plans, I first turned to a late edition of Beard's *The American Boy's Handy Book*. In that work, however, I discovered something interesting in the foreword. The modern edition, published in 1983, is a facsimile copy of an edition originally published in 1890 by Scribner. Noel Perrin writes in the foreword of the 1983 edition a suggestion that Daniel Carter Beard could have been the fictional character Huckleberry Finn, or, as portrayed by Mark Twain, an exaggeration of the real thing.

There were millions of American boys somewhat like him. That is, resourceful, adventurous, not much interested in school, very interested in wild places... In 1850, such a boy was born in Ohio. He was not the son of a small-town drunk, like Huck, but the son of a distinguished artist. His father was a Cincinnati painter who had many commissions in New York, and he himself was condemned to much boyhood stiflement in city houses. Just not full-time. A good part of his childhood he spent on a farm near Painesville, and that was the part that really counted. Here, like any savage, he could live by his own resources. All he needed was a jackknife, some twine, and few fishhooks in the lining of his hat, and ax, and he could fend for himself all summer.

That boy was, of course, Daniel Beard. Like other American boys, he tamed down somewhat as he grew up. He became an artist and writer himself, he got married, he even voluntarily lived sometimes in cities. But he never ceased cherishing the wild life of the woods, and he never ceased thinking it was the best possible life for boys. Both as a founder of the scouting movement and as a writer and illustrator of books, he devoted most of his life to trying to make the wilderness available to them.

Perrin's suggestion does not go so far as to say that Daniel Beard *is* Huckleberry Finn but rather that Daniel Beard was just one of many boys who at the time behaved like Huckleberry Finn – wild, untamed, and full of adventure. At the same time, Mark Twain was known for basing his fictional characters on genuine people that he knew or recalled from his life experience. When Mark Twain was asked directly of whom the 'real'

Huckleberry Finn was based, Twain answered and reproduced the account in his autobiography.

On March 8, 1906, Twain mentions a letter he received asking about the original "Huckleberry Finn" and that if the character was based on a Captain Tonkray. Twain replied that Huckleberry Finn was based on Tom Blankenship whose father was known as the town drunkard.

> In Huckleberry Finn I have drawn Tom Blankenship exactly as he was. He was ignorant, unwashed, insufficiently fed; but he had as good a heart as ever any boy had. His liberties were totally unrestricted. He was the only really independent person – boy or man – in the community, and by consequence he was tranquilly and continuously happy and was envied by all the rest of us. We liked him; we enjoyed his society. And as his society was forbidden us by our parents the prohibition trebled and quadrupled its value, and therefore we sought and got more of his society than of any other boy's.

Even though Beard was not a character sketch for Twain's Huckleberry Finn, Beard and Twain collaborated famously on *A Connecticut Yankee in King Arthur's Court*. The work was difficult; Beard recalled, "I worked so hard and steadily on the illustrations for Mark Twain's *A Connecticut Yankee in King Arthur's Court* that when the pictures were finished I collapsed." However, Beard concedes that, "I had more fun making the drawings for that book than any other book I ever illustrated."

I made about four hundred illustrations in seventy working days. The first illustration was that of a knight with lance set charging on the Yankee, who was climbing a tree. This pleased Mr Clemens very greatly. In the corner of the illustration there is a helmet as a sort of decoration with the visor partly open, of which Mark said, 'The smile on that helmet is a source of perennial joy to me.' When I finished the book he wrote, "Dear Mr Beard – Hold me under everlasting obligations. There are a hundred artists who could have illustrated any other of my books, but only one who could illustrate this one. It was a lucky day I went netting for lightning bugs and caught a meteor. Live forever."

On their mutual admiration of each other, Beard says of Twain that his humor, "like his character, was a product of his environment. Someday he will be remembered as a great philosopher who camouflaged his philosophy so that the public would understand it. It cannot be truly said that he administered sugar-coated pills, for some of his medicine was far from candied." Twain equally admired Beard when he commented, "Dan Beard is the only man who can correctly illustrate my writings, for he not only illustrates the text, but he also illustrates my thoughts."

Perhaps it is this synergy between Beard and Twain that gives the same sense that Noel Perrin felt in believing that Huckleberry Finn was an exaggeration of the real thing, and that the real thing was Daniel Beard. Where Twain fictionalized the untamable boy in Huckleberry Finn along the Mississippi River, it was Daniel Beard and his childhood friends who lived out these adventures along the Licking River.

The Civil War

According to his autobiography, when Daniel Carter Beard was 11 years old in 1861, he was too young to enlist in the Union Army, even as a drummer boy. His older brother Frank, on the other hand, "went to Painesville to enlist in the 7th Ohio Regiment, but on account of his defective hearing he was not accepted. He went to the 7th Regiment, however, as a special artist for Frank Leslie's illustrated paper." Of the work of these special artists, Beard continues to say,

> To the select few who have preserved collections of the envelopes, letterheads and printed cartoons of the Civil War it is no news to say that a really good history of the War Between the States was written in picture graphs and that time.

Rather than participating in the Civil War, Beard contented himself with boyhood games and mischief, often to the point of playing war games with real guns, shooting rocks and tacks at his friends or 'enemies' across the Licking River. At times, his mischief went a little too far, and caused Union Soldiers to keep extra watch along the banks of the river because, to the soldiers, Beard's war games sound much like real war.

As the Civil War waged on, young Daniel with his cousin Tom and Dick formed their own drum and fife band. As Beard recalls, "My cousin Tom had a drum, and my cousin Dick had a real fife; so there was nothing left for me to do but to play the bass drum." In front of the recruiting tent at the 5th street market place, "you might have seen three boys in front of that tent, pride oozing out of every pore of their skins as they played 'Yankee Doodle' and other similar airs."

1882

Returning to Noel Perrin's foreword of Beard's *The American Boy's Handy Book*, Perrin notes that Beard's book which originally appeared in 1882 "began as a series of articles for the old *St. Nicholas* magazine, designed to encourage city boys to recover their natural independence and self-sufficiency." Based on Perrin's statement, I originally thought that Beard published the plans for the Uncle Enos banjo as part of *St. Nicholas* magazine.

Searching For the Uncle Enos Banjo

Searching through an archive of the *St. Nicholas* magazine does not immediately reveal that Beard wrote an article with any semblance of that title, however, although Beard did write for *St. Nicholas*. It is certain, however, that the plans for the Uncle Enos Banjo were printed in *The American Boy's Handy Book* as supplementary material in the rear of the book which wasn't made available, officially, until 1890. But could they have been published earlier?

Following Daniel Carter Beard's studies to become an artist and engraver for clues to the origin of the Uncle Enos Banjo, he mentions that he studied art at night while he "wrote and illustrated for *St Nicholas, Harper's Round Table, Youth's Companion, Wide Awake* and other similar publications" After selling his first picture to *St Nicholas*, Beard's course as a professional artist and writer was set. He followed in the footsteps of his father and brothers.

I began to draw on wood for *Forest and Stream* and similar magazines. The old-fashioned way of making an illustration was to draw 'from your head,' and anybody who did not have the ability to sit down and draw offhand was not considered an artist. As for myself, I was still learning to draw. I visited the department stores and made sketches of their different objects of merchandise, which I later drew on wood for their published catalogues. I drew everything. Horatio Harper asked me to make some book-cover designs, which proved so successful that I was flooded with orders from all the prominent publishing houses and could have developed a lucrative profession as a book-cover designer. All this work was done for money, to enable me to become an illustrator like my brothers. In order to realize this idea I used the money that I made during the daytime to pay for my expenses at the Art Student's League night class.

For a number of years I worked as staff illustrator for *Cosmopolitan.* I worked as a regular contributor to the *St Nicholas* magazine. I had departments in the *Ladies' Home Journal,* the *Woman's Home Companion,* the *Pictorial Review* and the *American Boy.* I occasionally contributed to *Harper's Weekly, Harper's Young People* and acted as special artist for *Frank Leslie's Illustrated Weekly* on various occasions. On one occasion my name appeared as a contributor in five different publications for the current month.

Beard's work as both writer and illustrator was far reaching. The Uncle Enos Banjo plans could feasibly be made from any one of the publications that he wrote for. As for the origin of Beard's Handy Book in which the plans eventually appear Beard mentions:

> At my brother James's suggestion I collected the articles I had written for St Nicholas magazine, enlarged them and added a lot of new material, then submitted the manuscript to Charles Scribner's Sons, who at that time occupied a place on Broadway... After it was published I was pleased with the reviews.

Beard's Handy Book was published many times over the years following 1882, but it is not until the 1890 edition of the Handy Book that the Uncle Enos Banjo appears in the supplemental material added to the original 1882 edition. There is a clue in the supplemental material where Beard gives a copy of the expanded Handy Book as a Christmas gift in the year before its release - 1889. This suggests that the Uncle Enos Banjo plans actually dated between 1883 and 1889 – after his work for the *St Nicholas* magazine and before the publication of his Handy Book in 1890.

1884

Eventually, my search for the Uncle Enos banjo led me to find that Daniel Beard published *Christmas Eve with Uncle Enos* in *The Book Buyer Christmas Annual* which includes plans to build an Uncle Enos Banjo. [See Historic Cigar Box Instrument Plans]

Several curious observations emerge about the bound volume of *The Book Buyer* from 1884: it is uncertain if both November and December issues were combined, or if when the entire year of 1884 was bound in book form that the December cover was discarded. To discard a cover of a monthly publication when sent to binding was not uncommon.

Beard's Illustration of a Completed Uncle Enos Banjo

The critical difference between *Christmas Eve with Uncle Enos* as published in 1884, and the plans for *How to Build an Uncle Enos Banjo* published in 1890 is that the former actually comprises a story followed by the plans. When the plans are published again in 1890 the story was omitted.

The *Christmas Eve with Uncle Enos* story begins with the ignoble words, "Tom, Dick, and Harry were sitting around a big, blazing wood fire in a log farmhouse one Christmas morning, when their attention was attracted by the shuffling of feet and the thumping of a banjo." Before knowing the source of the commotion, the three boys continue to comment about Uncle Enos and the fact that he had broken his banjo, or that it had it fallen to pieces. They even recall that Uncle Enos's banjo was made from a gourd and that the banjo sounds they heard now were not from a gourd instrument. When Uncle Enos joins the boys inside to sit by the fire and to play a song on the banjo, the boys kept time by clapping their hands and stamping their feet. Afterwards, the boys are incredulous that Uncle Enos has made the banjo from a cigar box and a broomstick, a bit of an old shoe and a piece of clapboard. *Christmas Eve with Uncle Enos* continues with some racist events and comments, by today's standards, eventually to return to a scene where the three boys and Uncle Enos are listening to and examining the cigar box banjo. Without warning or transition, the story abruptly changes to the plans for How to Build an Uncle Enos Banjo which would eventually find their place in the 1890 edition of Beard's. *The American Boys Handy Book.*

Did Daniel Beard popularize the use of the three generic male names Tom, Dick, and Harry? While I didn't expect the connection or that possibility, it is plausible that Beard's cousins are two of the three characters that begin the story of "*Christmas Eve with Uncle Enos.*"

Beard, in his autobiography, often speaks of Tom Champlin, Dick Disney, and Harry Lendrum and their misadventures on the banks of the Licking River. The only remaining main character from that story, from which the Uncle Enos Banjo plans originally appeared, is Uncle Enos. Did Uncle Enos actually exist? Luckily, in his autobiography, Beard also mentions him among other freed African-American slaves.

> Anticipating the victory of the North, the colored people had flocked to the Union lines from all quarters and were known by everybody as

contrabands. These colored people were jovial, innocent and carefree. They would come to one's house and hunt a place in the summer kitchen, barn or any shelter where they could lodge. Then, without more ado, they would proceed to do the housework. Their wages consisted of their board. Everybody's house was full of colored help.

At our house we had Uncle Enos, a splendid, big, burly Negro, who as a slave was worth all of three thousand dollars, and his wife, Aunt Liza, equally valuable. However, free, they did not long retain their value. They had never before had an opportunity to buy and drink whisky, so whisky killed them both in a very, very short time.

Such freedom given to older slaves was not uncommon. Beard also remembers Uncle Cassius and his wife Aunt Annie.

They were a delightful old couple, formerly slaves. When they were too old to work they had been given their freedom to save expense to their owners. Being free and not being able to work meant that somebody must provide them with food, and this was done partly and cheerfully by the boys of the neighborhood.

Aunt Annie and Uncle Cassius were great favorites. Their minds were full of the lore of the old plantation – stories of hants, of ghosts and of graveyard rabbits whose hind feet were good-luck charms. This old couple could also sing many forgotten plantation melodies and some spirituals, untainted and unspoiled by efforts to make them conform to the white man's idea of music.

1885

The Oshkosh Daily Northwestern, March 9, 1885 published a review of Daniel C. Beard's book and a reprint of Uncle Enos Banjo Plans. This same copy appears again in *The Agitator: Wellsboro PA*, September 7, 1886.

> In a famous book for young people called "What To Do and How To Do It," Mr. Daniel C. Beard tells us how "Uncle Enos" constructed a home-made banjo. The boys will like to hear about it. Why not the girls, too, in these days when girls are beginning to find that they have hands, and hands that can learn the use of tools and make exquisite wood carvings and many other things? Uncle Enos was an old black man who had been a slave. He played very sweetly on a banjo made of "a cigar-box, a broom stick, a bit of an old shoe and a piece of clap-board."

I am not sure of what to make of these two newspaper reviews, apparently of *The American Boy's Handy Book*, but called by its subtitle *What to Do and How to Do It*. While the review does follow the publication of the first edition of Beard's Handy Book in 1882 and its reprints, and the review follows *Christmas Eve with Uncle Enos* which appeared in 1884, I have studied a copy of the Handy Book from 1888 which shows no sign of Uncle Enos or of the cigar box banjo. While an early edition of Beard's Handy Book did contain the appendix, it is more likely that the review is incorrectly referring to both the Handy Book and the Christmas Eve with Uncle Enos published at the end of 1884 in the Book Buyer, as if they were published together.

1890

Plans for *How to Build an Uncle Enos Banjo* are published by Beard in the appendix of the second edition of *The American Boy's Handy Book*. Originally these plans were published in *The Book Buyer Christmas Annual* in 1884 (and dubiously published in Beard's Handy Book again given the book reviews published in 1885 and 1886). The true second edition of *The American Boy's Handy Book* arrived in 1890 and included the first edition plus an appendix of supplemental material collected in response to the first edition.

Elevation of the Banjo

As I think more about Daniel Carter Beard's cigar box banjo plans and the fact that they were presented in the story of *Christmas Eve with Uncle Enos*, I consider that Uncle Enos is an older, former slave and that on Christmas Eve he is heard playing a banjo which he constructed. The three children, Tom, Dick and Harry, hear the sounds of Uncle Enos' playing at a distance. Uncle Enos is invited into their log cabin, and through the course of the story, he receives gifts from the boys. Uncle Enos only has the creation of his banjo and the time he spends with the children to give back – it was a gift of his time to provide the opportunity to listen to his singing, and to give the children the audience of his playing. The children scrutinize how the banjo is constructed and ultimately, what these boys observed and measured from looking at the Uncle Enos banjo is written down by Daniel Carter Beard as a set of plans for other young boys to create a similar instrument of their own.

Daniel Carter Beard's story of Uncle Enos sharing his homemade banjo to three children was a sign of the times in the 1880s. Between 1860 and 1880 the banjo, which had been previously viewed as a purely African instrument, became a fad among young women in the upper classes. In his story *Christmas Eve with Uncle Enos*, Beard captured the essence of this movement of the banjo from its earthy beginnings as an African slave instrument to something that was invited into the higher levels of society. This transition was not immediate though; the banjo still had to endure blackface minstrelsy, medicine shows, and an association with grog houses.

With the banjo's elevation into high-society and into the parlors of the upper class, it is not surprising that renowned music teacher Satis Coleman should begin her book, *Creative Music for Children*, describing her thoughts as she sits in her parlor plucking the strings of a banjo and reminiscing about her musical education as a child. Unlike Daniel Carter Beard who always had a healthy sense of child and retained some sense of being a little savage, it would take Coleman time to shed her traditional music training in order to reform how she taught her own group of child students. Starting her students out as little savages with the most basic of rhythms and single-string instruments, developing 3-note songs on cigar box violins and coconut banjos that the children made, they would ultimately grow into becoming a musician from the inside out. From little savages, Coleman's young students learned from experience, experimenting and growing with each new challenge, much like Daniel Carter Beard had in his youth on the banks of the Licking River.

Satis Coleman

"Imagination is more important than knowledge"
- Albert Einstein

Born in Tyler, Texas on June 12, 1878, Satis Coleman learned the violin and piano at an early age. Her own experience with music reminds me of my own when she describes in *Creative Music for Children* her first piano lesson at age eight: "Soon I would understand that mysterious array of black and white keys, and be able to manipulate them in a 'really truly' tune!" Coleman was disappointed from the onset because rather than being instructed to press a key and play "Yankee Doodle," she was confronted with a "picture like a fence, with many black spots on it."

Coleman, even at the early age of eight, was frustrated by needing to first learn to read music before actually playing it, an act that to her was much like teaching a child to read before they could speak. Coleman adhered to the regimen of playing the notes off the staff and was discouraged from her experiments to "play by ear" by her teacher. She "felt the deprivation very keenly."

After her first year of lessons, Coleman's piano lessons were discontinued. The reason for the termination of lessons is unknown, but she did continue to play the piano and experimented both playing by ear and reading notes to grow in musical feeling and understanding.

By 1917, Coleman had experimented, based on her own childhood memories, with developing a teaching method for children where their interaction with music was more fundamental and "a more joyous experience." In 1920 *Musical America* and *Good Housekeeping* published articles written by visitors to Coleman's music studio. Her teaching, as told in these articles, was fascinating for the amount of prowess that the young students possessed. They sang, danced, and played their own compositions much to the delight of the visitors. Coleman had been able to show the importance of teaching the meaning of the music before teaching a student the symbols for it. Additionally, Coleman observed that once her students improvised and experienced enough, that they were naturally drawn to learning notation in order to express more. In that moment, her students' motivation grew beyond their present capability and they were eager to learn more.

The Idea

Coleman makes an important distinction to the act of listening to music as opposed to creating it when she wrote, "we believe that we love music, but as a rule we do not love it enough to take the trouble to make it, and most of our home music at present is 'reproduced' and not 'home-made'."

> After a time, however, a problem arose: a few children wanted to play whose hands were too small and too weak to get any real satisfaction at

the piano. They wanted to play real tunes, and yet their fingers were not ready for it. For a long time, I had believed the children did not seek knowledge or any kind of training until they were mentally and physically ready for it, but here were some apparent exceptions. Why did these children have the impulse to play and insist on playing before they could manipulate one finger without all the others getting in the way? Drums and other time beating instruments which they had used did not answer-they wanted to play *tunes*. I was greatly puzzled.

The solution of my problem came most unexpectedly at the suggestion of friends, I gave below an exact account of the train of thought which led to that solution.

One morning in the midst of spring house cleaning, I dropped into a chair to rest for a moment and gather strength for a fresh attack. Things were piled about the room, and within reach of my hand was one of those long old-fashioned minstrel banjos, leaning against a chair. I lifted it to my lap and idly twanged the strings. There is something very appealing in the sound of gut strings stretched over parchment-something at once a lament and happy abandon-and when one can add to that sound a few childhood memories of Old Uncle Joe and the other darkies on Saturday evenings in a sunnier clime than this, the banjo claims a place of affectionate regard.

The monotonous chords soon worked a charm and I was surprised to see how quickly my aching fatigue disappeared. It had been quite a common habit for me to 'rest myself' from physical fatigue by playing the piano, but I had never experienced such a quick restoration as this. 'What is it in this instrument,' I wondered, 'that gives it so much power? Is it the peculiar tone quality, or what is it?'

'What is it,' I questioned, in this instrument that strikes so deeply and clings so tenaciously to the very roots of his nature? And why is it that, as I sit here stroking these strings, I am even more soothed than by piano playing, though I play the piano better, and have played it many years longer? Perhaps my position has something to do with it? No, my piano chair is just as comfortable as this, and my left arm is less relaxed than it is at the piano, so it can't be my position. Neither can this lively tune the responsible. Can it be the fact that I am holding the instrument so close to my body that my nerves take up the vibrations more perfectly, having contact with the vibrating instrument at the waist, both thighs and wrists and the fingers, as well as the sound waves through the ear? Surely that must have something to do with it. Then, there must be a difference between striking the string indirectly by means of a hammer, and striking and directly with your fingers. To feel with your fingers, a string vibrating in response to your own physical touch, gives a far greater pleasure than the use of a mechanism ever so perfectly devised for striking strings. You have produced a tone that is more truly your own. And so it seems to me that one who plucks the strings with one's fingers, will feel a closer intimacy with the instrument than one whose stroke must pass through a series of mechanical devices before the sound is made.

That's it! It's the *intimacy* of this thing! No keys, no hammers, sockets, or pins. Only the string, my fingers, and a resonating body beneath them! A direct touch and an instantaneous response! If that is the secret, then the banjo is not the only instrument that has the magic charm.

The fact that Coleman is playing the banjo in such a way in her description, hints at a movement that was taking place at the turn of the 19th to the 20th centuries. Namely, makers and teachers such as S.S. Stewart were actively trying to associate the banjo with higher classes. In "The Elevation of the Banjo" as referred to in *That Half Barbaric Twang: The Banjo in American Popular Culture* by Karen Linn,

> S. S. Stewart proudly announced in 1885 of the banjo was catching on in England with leading aristocrats, in France it was being introduced, and 'in Russia, the banjo only awaits competent teachers to introduce it to the nobility.' Albert Bauer had suggestions on how the banjo's image could be elevated.

> In a former letter, I spoke of 'elevating' the banjo and expressing it in that way I did not intend to impress upon the reader that it was necessary to play a high or difficult grade of music. There is a far better way of elevating instruments and to play difficult music on it. Take it into good company and keep it there. The more refined and intellectual the company the better it will be, and the longer and firmer hold it will take. The advance of the banjo began when it was taken up by the ladies, and by them introduced into the home circle. Before that it was heard most frequently in bar-rooms and out-of-the-way

places, with an occasional glimpse of it on the minstrel stage, coupled with a grotesque impersonation of a plantation negro. In that age of the banjo it was never heard in the drawing room or around the fireside. I was in New York four years and a half and gave lessons to hundreds of pupils, most of them among the wealthiest and most fashionable families in the city.

Of course Albert Bauer, like most banjoists of the time did not learn in such delicate surroundings. His first remembrance of the banjo was at a minstrel show at the Bowery theater, and he learned to play from some old timers who met in an upstairs room on Fulton Street. Bauer was a 10-year-old runaway working in a bookbindery at the time. In another column he reminisces about playing in barrooms with Lou Brenner, a talented old-timer whose barroom visitations led to an early alcoholic death. Bauer goes on to warn young teachers that 'the patrons of the banjo today are [of] the most refined and select circles of society, who would not for a moment tolerate the aroma of a grog shop in their presence. By catering to the tastes of the most enlightened people in his community and winning their approbation, he advances the banjo.'

References to old-time banjo players and alcohol consumption are not unusual. The Introduction included this story of how Picayune Butler lost the 1857 New York City banjo tournament due to his state of intoxication. Old-time professional banjo players were a mobile, rootless group that wandered in and out minstrel theater troupes and medicine shows, and if work could not be found, playing in the grog shop to bring in a little cash, at least enough to pay for drinks. By the second part of the nineteenth century, the temperance movement had greatly affected the drinking behavior of most Americans, but the socially liminal old-time banjo player remained unreformed, and became an embarrassment to the new generation of banjo players. In the desire to truly uplift their favorite instrument, some banjoists eschewed the roving life of the stage and settled down to a more respectable lifestyle as teachers of the banjo and local recitalists.

By the 1890s a new generation of professional players had come up who had never been part of the old-time social context, but the players and the teachers, who were the pioneers for a higher-class banjo in the 1880s, seemed never to have been fully reformed. They had to remind one another not to arrive at the homes of their new-found patrons with the smell of the grogshop on their breath, and they still traded stories about old times in theater troupes, medicine shows, and barrooms through the pages of the 1880s banjo journals. Even S. S. Stewart took a break from his banjo reform work to write a dime novel (a genre associated with the working class) about a young banjoist who plays in medicine and minstrel shows. Banjoists wanting to elevate their instrument, not only had to fight the stereotype image of the black man; one senses that they had to wrestle with themselves.

In the 1880s, the picture is one of male banjo teachers, secretly tugging on their starched collars, and female students, young 'society ladies' who liked to tie ribbons on their banjos, learning to play passably well some of the popular tunes of the day. Serious-minded banjoists acknowledged their debt to upper-class women for allowing them into refined circles, while at the same time complaining that these same women did not really take their studies very seriously.

Coleman did take her studies seriously, regardless of the instrument. Once she was struck with the idea of the intimacy of the tones of the banjo, with her fingers directly in contact with the strings to make a tone, she further recalls from her childhood:

> My older brother used to sit and play his guitar by the hour in the evening 'just resting himself' after working hard on the farm all day. He didn't know much about it – had picked up a few chords, a Spanish Fandango and one or two other little things – and not until this moment have I ever appreciated his point of view when he declined to study piano, for he loved the piano, and I had implored him to let me teach him what I knew. But he remained content to play his small guitar repertoire over and over again every evening. In those days, I rather pitied his poor musical taste, and felt that he did not really appreciate my revered instrument nor his opportunity to learn it. But now I see that his taste was wholesome and natural, and I respect his judgment in adopting an instrument that gave him the greatest return for the time he had to spend upon it.

> What are our simple strings? The simplest form zither has no frets, and a separate string for each note, even simpler than the guitar or banjo... Several of them whose hands are too small and too weak for the piano are longing to make music of some kind with their hands, and they really

could pluck, one at a time, the strings of the zither. Plucked strings and a string for each note, lying flat on the table or in the lap. Could any instrument, the simpler for children to play?

Yes, there was the Greek lyre, perhaps the simplest of all forms of plucked strings. The logical thing would be for me to start my children with the lyre! If I could only get one! But alas! there are none to be had. Why, I'll *make* one and let my little ones play on that! But... Even that is not the beginning!

Coleman abstracts the idea of music education for children to its most basic level. In fact, much like Daniel Carter Beard thought of boys as little savages, Coleman too sought to focus on the savage, untamed nature of her young students.

Their first music [would] not [come from] the Greeks, but much, much further back, even to primitive man and the early savages. 'They shall build up their own art and experience the development of music from the beginning,' I said to myself. Being little savages, they can understand savage music. I shall find the child's own savage level, and lift him gradually up to higher forms; and he shall understand each stage as he reaches it, for his power will grow with it, and his work will always be at his own level. The natural evolution of music shall be my guide in leading the child from the simple to the complex; and we, with guidance, may probably often discover and cover in one lesson things that required generations for man, without guidance, to learn.

Primitive man made his own instruments, and so shall we make many of ours, too! How children will love making them, and of course any child will love to play an instrument that he is made!

The simplest stringed instrument is, perhaps, a *hunter's bow*. To make a bow and arrow and listen for the sound of the string as the arrow was shot, was our first work in strings. We called this a *tension bow*, because it gave us an opportunity to observe the effects of tension on the tone of the string. The children discovered that the greater the tension of the string the higher the pitch of the tone.

After studying the Greek lyre based on pictures and artifacts seen in the museum, Coleman and her students used a tortoise shell to create "the sound intensifier... a concave body" to construct a Greek lyre. Then, after this experiment, she continues to experiment with another familiar object.

If a concave surface was a good resonator wouldn't the box be equally good? To find out, we made a *box lyre*. For this we used a cigar box, with a hole in its cover and a strong frame around the box. On this lyre we used wire strings and the children found that their tones were louder than those of other strings we had used.

Although the classic lyre is more pleasing to the eye, the home-made box lyre is very satisfactory, and I see no reason why any boy or girl who can use tools should not have one of these simple home-made instruments.

Some historian said that when the lyre got a neck, the lute stage had come. We had used a cigar box with a hole in it for the box lyre. We took another cigar box, and instead of making a frame to support the strings, one long support was run through the center of the box and the strings attached to the end of the strip, running along almost the length of the strip. Although in the box lyre we had eight strings, in this instrument the strip was wide enough only for three peg holes in the top, so we could have only three strings. But luckily we didn't need any more, for when the strings were tuned the little bridges in place to keep the strings from rattling me against the strip of wood, we found that we could make other notes – in fact, we could finish the entire scale, by pressing fingers on the strings and making the parts that vibrated shorter and shorter. This was our *Cigar-box Lute.* The three strings were tuned to the major triad and the children found it easy to play chords as well as melodies on it.

The logical result of discovery of the use of the bow on a coconut banjo was the desire to make an instrument especially for bowing. The children were content to have only one string at first until they learned to use the bow with good results, for by this time they knew how to manipulate one string to produce several tones. Following the natural development of musical instruments, this new instrument was destined to be a *Monochord.* We used a large, deep cigar box, and put a strong stick through it; cut *f* holes (like other bowed instruments we had seen) and stretched a violin D string over a high bridge. In the last stages we were almost breathless with the impatience to see what the monochord's tone would be. Finally it was ready to speak for the first time, and we stood around it in ceremonious awe. Its maker (a little girl of eight), radiant with excitement, drew the bow slowly across the string... and there on the workbench lay that wonderful singing Thing, ready to give out its voice to any child who wished to draw the bow across it. No other instrument we had made had been quite the revelation that this one was. There seemed something quite human about it, and the children danced around it in ecstatic glee, taking turns at trying its tone. We found that the easiest way to play the instrument was to hold it firmly between the knees. This gave room for free arm movement.

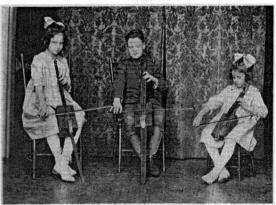

Three of Coleman's Students, including Charles, "A Cello and Two Monochords Serve This Trio in Their Chamber Music Combinations"

[Inspired by the monochord,] Charles (age nine) would go even further and make an instrument with three strings to be played upon with the bow. He would make a *cigar-box cello* out of the biggest cigar box he could possibly find! The cello proved as satisfactory as the monochord, and its three strings made its possibilities greater. Many three-stringed cellos were made in the studio, of varying sizes and with great varieties of tone. The deep cedar-wood cigar boxes seemed to give the best tone.

1920

The June 1920 issue of *Good Housekeeping* included an article which becomes the primary source for *Creative Music for Children*, published in 1922. A similar (or perhaps the same article) is also published in *Musical America*.

Creative Music for Children

From her successes in musical teaching by her own theories, *Creative Music for Children* by Satis Coleman was published in 1922. Many examples of instruments made from boxes, birds nests, with illustrations exist in her work. Coleman makes an excellent example of the desire to learn and to play, in both senses of the word. There is also an example of a student replacing the inferior cigar box violin with a "real" violin. However, the real violin was an inspiration to create a better box version of a violin by another student.

> Elizabeth was the first to attempt a violin to be held at the shoulder. She found a small flat cigar box, and following, with my assistance, the same plan that was employed in making the cellos, she soon had a *cigar-box violin* which she could hold under her chin and play – real violin fashion! This instrument also had three strings. It seemed to me

that four strings would make playing a little too difficult for children until after they had acquired some experience in the use of an instrument with strings that were more easily separated than four strings could be.

The holding of the instrument and the proper use of the bow seemed, to my mind, hard enough at first, without having undue complications in keeping the bow from striking more than one string at a time. However, since they had used the bow on the monochord and cello, its use in the violin position did not present any great difficulty, and three strings were easily managed. The cigar box violin was tuned in fifths (as were the cellos). After Elizabeth had tried out her new violin and played a few melodies on it, she spontaneously hugged it to her, saying, "Oh, I just love this little fiddle!" The fiddle was truly hers, for she had made it. Of course she loved it.

This little violin served as a model for other children to follow. The musical possibilities of these instruments were patiently investigated by their makers, who found that very pleasing results could be obtained.

As soon as there were two instruments to be played with a bow, the children were eager to play them together, and by the end of the second year of the experiment, we had a delightful quartet of home-made stringed instruments. This quartet played folk songs in unison and in four parts; classic melodies, and original compositions.

After a few months' use of her cigar-box violin, Santa Claus brought Elizabeth a "real" one, and this marked an important point in her musical development. She now had a professionally made violin in her hands for the first time in her life, and yet it seemed almost a well known friend. She not only knew at once the reason for every part of its construction, but was able to appreciate all the advantages it had over her own crude instrument: its fine polish, slender neck, graceful curves, and especially the "scooped out" places at the sides where the bow could have freer play.

The instrument fell naturally into place under her chin, and when she drew her bow across it for the first time, she was conscious of the richness and fullness of tone which she had not been able to produce before and she marveled at the violin maker's skill. She possessed the background of knowledge and experience which gave her the ability to appreciate at once its finer tone quality and greater musical possibilities, and to discriminate between its own good and bad tones. Although nothing but a "real" violin of good make will now meet her musical needs, she still holds an affectionate regard for the object of her own handiwork – her first little violin.

When the time came for Margaret to make a violin, she wished to try to make one more nearly like the new violin which she had heard Elizabeth play. She used thin boards of Spanish cedar wood, and made the box instead of using a cigar box, for she thought that a deeper box might have a fuller tone, so she made it just deep enough to fit under her chin without the use of a chin rest.

A peep into the "real" violin showed a sound post to intensify the sound. She decided to try a sound post also and see what happened. A little round post was glued to stand behind the bridge under the smallest string, and under the largest string, a small sounding board was glued to the box cover. The effect of these additions was very pronounced, and Margaret's violin proved to be a definite step in advance of the simpler cigar box fiddles. Its tone quality and power make this instrument worthy of a place beside many of professional make.

Trapezoidal Violin

The idea of a box-shaped violin and its worthiness was not a new concept, in 1922. Felix Savart, a 19th-centruy

French physicist, experimented with trapezoidal-bodied or 'rational' violins as early as 1819 when he published his work *Mémoire sur la construction des instrumens à cordes et à archet* in Paris. And though Savart's rational violins never really found their place in popular use, his work was vindicated in 1884 by Edward Heron-Allen in his work *Violin-Making, As it Was and Is* where he describes:

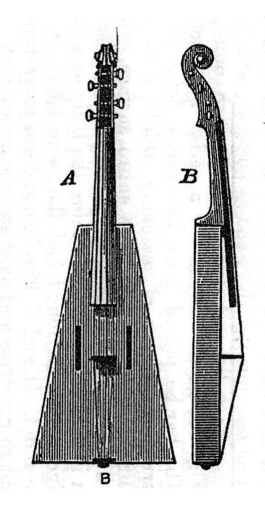

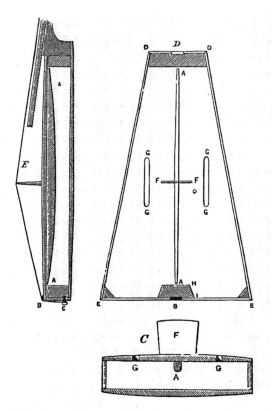

*The Felix Savart Trapezoid Violin as Illustrated in 1885 by
Ed Heron-Allen*

Savart's Trapezoid Violin or Box-fiddle was one
of the most celebrated and satisfactory
experiments ever tried on the construction of the
instrument. He was led to its production by a
series of carefully conducted experiments, which
went to prove – (1) that a plane surface vibrates
much more readily than an arched or curved one;
(2) that consequently there are points on the
surface of a violin of the ordinary form where the

vibrations are reduced to a minimum or cease altogether; (3) that the bouts, corner blocks, and *ff* holes are the principal causes of localities of this reduced vibration.

[The] trapezoid shape was not founded particularly on any scientific reason, but that it being necessary to have a certain contained mass of air [approximate to that of a standard violin, and that] this shape was best adapted to give the instrument a narrowness at the bridge.

Arguing that the sound-holes of an ordinary violin are cut f-shaped only, so as to counteract the resistance the curved surface offers to the vibrations, this necessity being absent in the Savart fiddke, he cut his sound-holes straight... to cut as few fibres of the wood as possible.

Edward Heron-Allen mentions in a footnote that an excellent resume of this memoir appears at in the *Penny Magazine* of June 30th 1838, entitled, "How to Make a Cheap Violin." Consulting this memoir we can follow Savart's early experiments and observations. His first observation is that older violins acquired a resident or vibrating character through age, which new instruments did not possess. His second observation is that the construction of the violin was never scrutinized from a scientific point of view. Savart investigated the sources of sound to determine what were or were not essential parts of the instrument. Savart separated his experiments into segments: first, he tested of the curvature of the face of the violin which he determined failed to "contribute to the sonorous effect." Second, he conducted a series of tests with violins made with flat surfaces. He studied the bridge, which rested on the surface of the violin with two little feet. He examined the sound post, which served as a support to the upper surface, but also as a means to transfer vibration to the lower surface, and he studied its placement with respect to the bridge. He examined the brace bar or *bar of harmony* and its placement with respect to the bridge. He examined the size and shape of the f-holes on either side of the bridge and opted instead for a simpler straight pair of slits in his design. And lastly he studied the body shape of traditional violins and replaced the complicated curved and bent sides with straight sides to form the trapezoid violin.

As odd as the Savart violin appears, the success of his experiments were demonstrated, as was customary in France at the time, in front of the Academy of Sciences who invited the chief of the orchestra of the *Théâtre Feydeau* to play Savart's instrument, as well as the violin he normally played. The violinist was placed in a different room from the listeners and directed to play the same piece on both violins; in other words, the chief of the orchestra was listening blind. As the blind listening continued, the new violin was found to possess a greater purity of tone and a more perfect equality between different tones. The Academy of Sciences commission could not tell the difference between the two violins or a marginally preferred the trapezoidal violin claiming that it had "a little more sweetness of tone."

1939

If the box fiddle as an inferior instrument was still a concern, it should be noted that even with non-traditional woods and construction methods, it is the skill of the maker which gives the instrument its tone. An excellent example of this comes from the account of Frank E. Coulter, who created a selection of violins each made with different woods, and had them performed to an audience in a "Dark Room." According to the interview with Coulter in *American Life Histories: Manuscripts from the Federal Writers' Project*:

> I've always been musical and a natural mechanic… the best thing I could do was to develop the very finest stringed musical instruments that could be made. Of course that meant first, the violin. The tone of the violin has always been high-pitched. What I wanted to do was to develop an instrument of powerful tones. Along about 1910 an immense change in the world of music began to be noticeable. It was then the standard pitch began to go down…

> With the advent of the radio, music changed. The high soprano voice and the high-pitched instruments, like the mandolin and the banjo, are no good on the radio. You never hear the shrill-voiced old Italian violin any more. The most popular instruments today are the saxophone and the double-bass viol.

> There's no good or bad wood in making musical instruments. Any wood is all right. It's the way you use it. It is all nonsense, that talk of special wood from Europe. Appearance now counts for a lot, too. I won $450 once on a wager. I was to make three violins, one of standard material, one from a dry-goods box – Ontario tamarack – and the third from a camphorwood chest. The judges were to listen to each of them being played in the dark, and [try to] notice any difference – know

when the violins where changed... I won the bet. They couldn't detect any difference in the tone of those three violins, and they bought them for $150 each. That was the wager.

Rapid Prototypes

The idea of distilling a complex and curved musical instrument down to the most basic of shapes and the most basic of materials is not a technique relegated to the late 19th century and early 20th century. In 2006 R.M. Mottola wrote an article for *American Lutherie* entitled *A Method from Generating Rapid Prototypes of the Flattop Guitar*. In that article, Mottola sought to be as objective as possible when experimenting with instrument prototypes. Mottola recognizes the main problem with being objective, stating:

> Objectivity is a highly desirable quality of experimental investigation, although it may be impossible to fully achieve... particularly when [your] own work is involved. The general research scenario goes something like this; a hypothesis is developed, usually involving some structural change thought to be beneficial. The instrument is built, the experiments are run and the results are analyzed to see if they support the original hypothesis or not.

> Given the time and personal effort and expense involved in producing the instruments. It is all too easy for me to strum a few times and declare it to be a success, glossing over or entirely skipping all the important running of the experiments. After

all, it sounds good. It's beautiful. It has its own voice.

In Mottola's view, the idea of a violin guitar or banjo made from a cigar box would be an ideal prototype instrument. Mottola continues to praise the prototypes adding that they possess certain desirable qualities:

> They are easy to make modifications to... But probably the most important quality of all is that despite all of their obvious shortcomings as instruments, these prototypes sound close enough in tone to the real instruments they attempt to emulate so that the meaningful information can be gleaned from them.

> The overall length of the bodies is the same the width of the base of the trapezoidal body is the same as the widest part of the lower bout of the traditional body. Finally the shoulders of the trapezoidal body are wide enough so that the area of the traditional body is outside the sidelines of the trapezoidal body at the upper bout is approximately equal to the difference between the bodies at the waist. This makes for a prototype body that includes his approximately the same amount of air and has roughly equivalent plate area as the traditional body that it is intended to emulate.

Mottola, in building prototype guitars from unconventional materials such as Formica and plywood, stresses the fact that the prototypes are similar in construction and embrace the most important elements of an instrument, even though they lack the curves and the grace of a traditional instrument: the trapezoidal body of the prototype contains approximately the same amount of air and has roughly the equivalent plate area as the traditionally shaped body that it is intended to emulate.

I greatly admire Mottola for his insights on trapezoidal shaped prototype guitars. It would seem that a cigar box with its simple box shape and the neck attached to it would easily qualify as one of these prototypes – be it a violin, banjo, ukulele, or guitar. In fact, considering cigar box instruments as a prototype does more to elevate their status than those efforts made by S. S. Stewart and Albert Bauer at the turn of the previous century to elevate the banjo to a parlor instrument accepted by the upper class.

Cigar box instruments have now an important new role, far beyond being considered just a child's toy or as a beginner instrument, or as a replacement for a traditional instrument when one could not be afforded or found or borrowed: the cigar box instrument serves as a quick and inexpensive way to test an instrument design. In such cases, the cigar box prototypes of traditional instruments were critical for experimentation and as an inexpensive means for stringed instrument makers to rapidly test a theory, make adjustments as needed, and then build another inexpensive prototype. Such prototyping is not unheard of in the modern era. In the 1960s, John Huber in the Martin Guitar Plant in Nazareth, Pennsylvania and Sam Kamaka Jr. in the Kamaka Ukulele factory in Honolulu, Hawaii experimented with similar instruments. However, whereas John Huber used Brazilian Rosewood, Spruce for the top and Rosewood for the fingerboard and bridge, Sam Kamaka Jr. used a selection of 1889 brand cigar boxes made from Western Cedar to craft a handful of the most distinctive cigar box ukuleles.

Sam Kamaka Jr.

*"If you make instruments
and use the family name,
don't make junk."*
- Sam Kamaka, Sr.

According to myth and legend, Sam Kamaka made twelve cigar box ukuleles from several Sam'l J. Davis y Ca 1886 brand cigar boxes early in his career. This story seemed like a fairytale beginning for Sam Kamaka whose family now is the sole remaining early makers of Hawaiian Ukuleles. Like most myths, there is some truth to the Kamaka story, but the details have been distorted to shade the whole truth. My search for facts started with Manuel Nunes, who according to the legend was Sam Kamaka's teacher.

In *The Ukulele A Visual History,* Jim Beloff begins the story with Manuel Nunes who, according to his advertisement, claimed the title of "inventor of the ukulele" in 1879. It is widely agreed that the birth of the ukulele can be traced from the specific date of August 23, 1879, the day that the *Ravenscrag,* a ship from Maderia, arrived in Hawaii. According to legend, passenger Joao Fernandez hopped onto the wharf and began playing a Portuguese instrument known as the *braguinha*, or *machete de braga*, which is still a popular four-string instrument in the Portuguese island of Madeira today.

The story of Sam Kamaka, Sr., again according to legend, begins with him as a student of Nunes who, according to Nunes' obituary in *The Modesto Evening News* August 2, 1922, suggests that "Manuel Nunes, inventor of the ukulele, dies in Honolulu. He built the first ukulele out of a cigar box in 1879."

It is plausible that Nunes would have trained his student to make ukuleles out of such humble materials. Again, legend hints at this, as Beloff states, "According to legend, Sam Kamaka tried to make ukuleles out of twelve cigar boxes. Out of the twelve boxes, Kamaka was able to make seven good ukes."

There are several problems with this fairytale story about Kamaka's early beginning as ukulele maker. Apart from Nunes claiming the title of "inventor of the ukulele," the rest of the story is pure conjecture.

First, to dispel the myth of Kamaka working for Nunes, "Pride and Pineapples," an article published in *The Fretboard Journal*, Number 10, 2008, states that:

> When Fred Kamaka Jr. thoroughly researched his family's business history, he found no verifiable evidence that his grandfather, Samuel Sr., ever worked for the legendary Manuel Nunes – dispelling a widely held story that he'd learned his craft working for that ukulele-making pioneer. Sam Sr. may have observed Nunes at work, but he learned instrument making most everywhere else, according to Sam Jr., 86, and Fred Sr., 83.

So if Sam Kamaka, Sr. *was not* a student of Nunes, when did he make the twelve cigar box ukuleles? Well, actually he didn't.

On a visit to their small shop at 550 South Street, in Honolulu Hawaii, I had the opportunity to ask about the cigar box ukuleles that were made by Kamaka. After talking to Fred Kamaka Sr., Fred Kamaka Jr., and Chris Kamaka, it became clear that what limited information I *thought* I knew about the few cigar box ukuleles was incorrect.

According to Fred Kamaka Sr., the cigar box ukuleles were not built by Sam Kamaka Sr., but rather by Sam Kamaka Jr. in the 1960s. Fred actually drifted off in mid-sentence when I asked him about the dates of the first cigar box ukulele, and after a brief phone call to his brother Sam Kamaka Jr., he confirmed that the first ones where not made until the 1960s. He continued by stating that there were about 60 cigar boxes around the shop and they appear to have been a nuisance for Fred, as he emphatically recollected asking Sam Jr., "What are you going to *do* with them all?" "He liked to experiment," Fred Sr. continued.

Sam Kamaka Sr. experimented with the ukulele's design when he started with the ukulele similar to those made by Manuel Nunes which were much thinner and narrower than the ukuleles of today. The early ukuleles based on the Portuguese *braguinha* had a very "feathery" sound. After Sam Kamaka Sr. studied how guitars were made and played by the Portuguese, Italian, and Spanish, he incorporated a much larger sound chamber for the now famous "Pineapple" ukulele. It was that ukulele that set the standard for what a Kamaka ukulele would sound like – much fuller sounding, with more resonance.

Listening to Fred Kamaka Sr. play the Pineapple ukulele #1, a modern figure-eight (guitar) shaped soprano ukulele, and a cigar box ukulele side-by-side, the similarities in tone were, in fact, amazing. In a blind test, I'm not sure that I could tell one from the other.

An early 1960's cigar box ukulele made by Sam Kamaka Jr. featuring a violin style neck and trapezoidal body

Sam Kamaka, Jr.

Returning to Beloff's account, "According to legend, Sam Kamaka [Jr.] tried to make ukuleles out of twelve cigar boxes. Out of the twelve boxes, Kamaka was able to make seven good ukes." When I showed the photographs of the cigar box ukuleles to Chris Kamaka, he surprised me when he explained that the cigar box ukulele's shown in Beloff's *The Ukulele A Visual History* are not actual Kamaka ukuleles because of the position of the hinges. The photographs in Beloff's book clearly show the hinges on the top. The Kamaka ukuleles always had the hinges on the back. Also, from the photographs, there does not appear to be any finish on the ukuleles. Fred Kamaka Sr., from the three examples I've seen, have the same seven coats of lacquer finish that their traditional ukuleles have.

The final nail in the coffin for the cigar box ukulele myth goes back to the obituary of Nunes that claimed "Manuel Nunes, inventor of the ukulele... built the first ukulele out of a cigar box..." I questioned both Jim Beloff and John King, two well-known and respected historians on the ukulele, about the possibility of a surviving Nunes cigar box ukulele. King responded:

> With regard to your question, does any other evidence of a Nunes cigar box ukulele survive today, the short answer is: none that I have seen. I would also be loath to characterize the obituary you mention as evidence of anything. The article you cite is likely a national wire story, as the death of Nunes was published in newspapers across the States, however the notices of his death in the two major Honolulu papers credit Nunes with the invention of the instrument and say nothing about cigar boxes. Nunes came to Hawaii in 1879, a

skilled artisan working in a field with a proud history in Madeira. As a *marceneiro*, or cabinet maker, he would have been familiar with the stringed-instrument making trade, borne out by his ad for furniture and stringed instruments in the Portuguese-Hawaiian weekly, *O Luso Hawaiiano*, in 1885. I have come across mention of cigar box instruments, usually on the Mainland – less frequently in Hawaii – and they are invariably credited to persons without the means to purchase an instrument rather than established makers. In that sense, Kamaka's cigar box ukes are exceptional. I seriously doubt they have any connection to a proto-cigar box Nunes instrument from 1879.

King is correct. As far as I know, no other traditional instrument maker in the world has dabbled in cigar box variants of their instruments, let alone sells them and continues to service and repair them, should they find their way back to the Kamaka factory.

Ukulele Stamps

Kamaka's continued success as ukulele makers is noted when on August 23, 2004 a stamp booklet celebrating the *125th Anniversary of the 'Ukulele* features three Kamaka ukuleles. While the stamps inside feature Manuel Nunes, the front cover shows 3 different ukuleles: The Sam Kamaka Sr. pineapple ukulele #1 (complete with pineapple paint job), a standard figure 8 (guitar shaped) ukulele, and a Sam Kamaka Jr. cigar box ukulele.

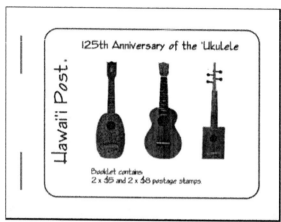

Three Historic Kamaka Ukuleles

The Cigar Box Violin

"Simplicity is the ultimate
sophistication"
-Leonardo da Vinci

I t is not too surprising that the majority of artifacts
on cigar box instruments fall in the violin category.
It is, after all, the longest lived instrument
compared to the banjo, ukulele, and guitar. The
violin and fiddle have long standing roots in the
European culture dating far back into the Middle Ages
and are shown in artwork and carvings from that era,
appearing frequently as a Rebec Fiddle, an early member
of the Viol family.

What I do find surprising, however, is the bulk of
information about cigar box violins in comparison to
every other type of cigar box instrument. Even as the
popularity of other instruments grew, none of those
instruments comes close to the magnitude of artifacts
about cigar box violins and fiddles. Perhaps cigar box
instruments were too common place or marginal to be
news worthy by the time other instruments were
fashionable.

Regardless of the reason, from the breadth of
information on the cigar box violin, a recurring theme in

cigar box instruments, whatever their form, is clear – the absolute most fundamental of all of these instruments is one that uses a single string combined with a cigar box and a broom handle to create the most basic of all instruments – the monochord. Another recurring theme in cigar box instruments is the stories of musicians that began their musical careers on cigar box contraptions as their first instruments. And, eventually, these musicians would graduate to a more traditional or proper instrument of the same kind. The cigar box variants that were made in their childhood are seldom mentioned again.

As times changed, the circumstances surrounding the cigar box violin also changed. It was adopted by performers in vaudeville. When vaudeville struggled and faltered, motion pictures and radio were there to catch the performers and their cigar box fiddles.

1861 to 1865

These four years span the American Civil War which ended with the 13th amendment and the emancipation of African slaves. A depiction, created by Edwin Forbes, of two Union soldiers with a cigar box violin exists for this time period as a sketch, the etching copyright date is 11 years later, 1876 [See Edwin Forbes].

Though more likely a reenactment of Civil War times given the presence of barbed wire (which wasn't patented as an invention until November, 1868) on the fence, the ensemble pictured shows a troupe of musicians, two of whom are seen playing cigar box violins. A third, on the far right, is seen playing a cello-like instrument that would have been made from packing crates, which were commonly reused as fuel for fires, shelter, or other makeshift objects needed by resourceful soldiers.

The Great Cigar Box and Packing Crate Ensemble

1883

In *The Perry Pilot* John Warford reports about a monochord, in this case bowed like a violin, and comments about the player's talents to create both music and other sounds.

OUT OF THE USUAL ORDER

Among the sights which were witnessed on the dock yesterday, the most noticeable was a man having a fiddle made of a cigar box, and having for a handle an old broomstick. There was only one string on the instrument, but he rendered the most difficult operatic selections with the greatest of ease. The music was very fine. He also gave imitations of various animals and also different instruments. A large crowd listened to the music. The musician himself was a thorough artist, having been connected with various theatres. — *Albany Press Knickerbocker.*

1885

Iowa State Reporter: Waterloo, August 20 1885 published a brief account of a cigar box violin in one man's collection of fine violins,

> Joseph Heine's genuine "Amatic" Violin, three hundred years old resented to him by a grandson of Baron Dayneville, of London, valued at $3000; his cigar box violin, presented to him by Mr. Hamlin, of the firm of Mason & Hamlin, Boston; and his scrap book, containing more than on thousand press notices from the leading papers of the world, will be on exhibition at Stanley's jewelry store, west side, Thursday afternoon.

ca 1887

An example of an eventually well-known musician that started on a cigar box violin and then graduated to a traditional version of the instrument is given in Larry Sitsky's book, *Music of the Twentieth-century Avant-garde: A Biocritical Sourcebook*, which mentions the brief account of Carl Ruggles (1876 – 1971) who with Edgard Varèse and Charles Ives were the standard bearers of the American atonal movement in the 1920s.

Born, Charles Sprague Ruggles, he was the second of three children. As a child Ruggles fashioned a violin from a cigar box [ca 1886 to 1888] which was soon replaced with a more conventional instrument donated by the local lighthouse keeper. Ruggles was apparently a gifted beginner as he played duets with Mrs. Grover Cleveland.

1887

The account of Sam Jackson's cigar box fiddle is the essence of simplicity as reported in *The Galveston Daily News*, May 17, 1887. Unlike most cigar box instruments mentioned elsewhere, Jackson's fiddle did not have tuning pegs to tension the strands of thread which served as strings.

SAM JACKSON'S FIDDLE.

A middle-aged colored man named Sam Jackson this morning strolled into The News branch office and struck up a tune on a fiddle of his own make. He knocked three or four tunes out of it, and hummed a monotonous refrain in a subdued tone. He said that be could sing much louder, but "De loud singin' would 'stroy de harmony made by de fiddle and de bow."

The body of the instrument was a flat cigar box. Nailed upon it was a rough pine stick that extended over one end, which answered the purpose of a handle. Along this handle were four strings. The two first were made of Clark's No. 8

thread and the two last of No. 12 thread. Each string had extra strands of thread. All these were strung over a thin bridge and were fastened at each end of the stick through the agency of slits. The threads at the end of the fiddle that rested on his shoulder were knotted. At the end where the keys should have been the threads were doubly waxed. To tune up he merely drew the threads that hang down from the handle. Each string had its separate - and distinct sound, like the strings of a violin.

The bow was a carved piece of hickory. Across this were stretched two strings twisted from No. 12 thread, and also waxed. In the top of the box were round holes. Although the sounds that came from Sam's fiddle were weak, they were delicate and clear. A violinist could have drawn sweet music from it.

"Do you make money out of your fiddle, Sam?"
"I makes a libbin' out of it."
"How?"
"I plays in s'loons and in de streets an' picks up consid 'able nickles. Den I plays at parties to' de culled folks."

Sam walked out of the branch office playing Old [Dan] Tucker and humming an accompaniment in a dreary way. He lives in the vicinity of the Sconewall engine house, on Smith street, and is fast becoming one of the public characters of the city.

Albert Leiff's Cigar Box Fiddle

The note accompanying this old cigar box violin reads, "Made by Clarence Bonnie for Albert Leiff when he was eight years old." Reading from the obituary of Florence and Fern Peterson, these twin sisters are noted as two remarkable women along with their uncle Albert Leiff for the gift of their charities to the communities of Alcester, Hawarden, and Akron. Their obituary mentions that their gift, "will keep giving for generations to come."

The Peterson obituary mentions that their uncle Albert Leiff lived to be 99 years old, passing away in 1978. Using Leiff's age and year in which he passed away, combined with his age from the note included with the cigar box violin. Simple arithmetic establishes that this cigar box violin was created in 1887.

1890

In 1890, Edwin Forbes published *Thirty Years After: An Artist's Story of the Great War*, including an etching of "Home Sweet Home" originally published in 1876 in *Life Studies of the Great Army*. In this new edition, Forbes added his recollection of the events surrounding the scene captured in the etching as well as adding another tailpiece etching of the violin being made. [See Edwin Forbes]

1896

From a detritomusicologist standpoint, this article from *The Galveston Daily News*, May 31, 1896, is a gold mine of information about several instruments made from discarded or leftover materials. The article is an account of an evening's festivities in a gold camp located by the Potaro River

POTARO COARSE, COARSE GOLD.

One man had a fiddle made cut of a cigar box, another a banjo similarly made, another an oil can with a string in it and the rest with tin plates and cans, which they beat upon with their fists. The "comfuman" appeared in the circle wrapped in a white blanket so that only his eyes showed, and-as he stepped into the circle the "music" began. It was a horrible noise—no tune, hut simply a beating of time on the tins—while the man with the fiddle sawed away on his own hook and the one with the oil can and the string made his instrument moan and groan In a most delightful manner.

Following the description of the "music" from the Potaro coarse gold camp, another hint that cigar box violin music was deemed sub-par comes from the parenthetically placed, sarcastic, punctuation in *The Sunday Light*, March 1, 1896, on the return of Bishop Forest,

CATHOLIC NEWS

During the reception of the cardinal Tuesday night, he was serenaded by Paulo Persia, Domenico Volino and Rocco Persia with their stringed instruments, and listened to such pleasing(?) Catholic music as "Garibaldi's March" and "Royal Italia." As an offset to this, they played "Il Trovatore." and Paulo Persia played "Schubert's Serenade" on his one stringed cigar box violin, which the cardinal afterward took in his hands, examined closely, and expressed surprise that so much music could be drawn from so simple an instrument.

ONE MAN'S TRASH

1902

From *The Davenport Daily Leader*, January 19, 1902, "Uncle Ned" tells of Reception of Mrs. Patrick Campbell. It's uncertain if fans rejoiced at the fact that Jan Kuelik's first violin was made from a cigar box for the humble beginnings of "genius" or if they are relieved that the cigar box violin is no longer played for its pleasing(?) "music."

> All the world delights in prodigies and in the miracles of genius, and hence a great stir is felt among the musically inclined, for the famous violinist, Jan Kubelik, now of age, is to play here this evening. Some go so far as to insist that he is a second Paganini. He is a Bohemian by birth and those delighting in romantic, will be rejoiced to learn that his father was a market gardener who made his son's first fiddle from a cigar box. The lad played on this instrument when he had reached the mature age of five years. Now he plays on a Stradivarius that cost $7,500, or on a Guarnerius price $5.000.

The Cigar Box Banjo

"The instrument proper to them is the Banjar, which they brought hither from Africa"
-Thomas Jefferson

Is it rebellion to question the ownership of objects like musical instruments, of their creation, or of the music that was played on them? If the words of Thomas Jefferson are taken in the context of the pre-emancipation South of 1781, there is a cold distance between the half-barbaric, savage music of the banjo and the ear of the Jeffersonian listener.

Nearly a century later, Paul Oliver references the musical abilities of escaped slaves in *Savannah Syncopators: African Retentions in the Blues*. To Oliver, reading "of a slave escaping with only his clothing and a violin, or attempting to carry with him both a violin and tambourine reveals much." To Oliver, the way in which musical instruments were prized possessions extended beyond their physical form. Even the memory of such an instrument was critical for the creation of a new one. Oliver continues: "A similar African lute with a gourd bowl has too been considered to be the source of Jefferson's banjar. Known as the bania, as Curt Sachs has noted in *Reallexikon der Musikinstrucmente*, not only its form but even in its name may have been transported to North America."

What I find ironic in the accounts of these musical slaves that Oliver writes about is that the slaves escaped from being treated as a possession and as a savage for the promise of a better urban life in the North, while Beard sought to teach the urban youth to escape their urban existence and return to becoming little savages.

1886

Originally published in *Harpers Young People* (Vol VII, Feb 23, 1886 pp 262-263), John Richards gives plans very similar to the Uncle Enos Banjo featured in Beard's book. Copies of these plans are also published in the March 25, 1886, *Waterloo, edition of the Iowa State Reporter* in that same year with credit given to John Richards and *Harpers Young People*. [See Historic Cigar Box Instrument Plans]

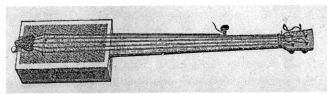

John Richards's Cigar Box Banjo

1891

Real picture postcards as part of the "C.T. Southern Pickaninny Scenes" are published. "The Blackville Serenade" is printed with two slightly different backgrounds. The same image is used with a third background entitled Darkies' Serenade, Florida. And again, it is published with what appears to be a cropped version of the same image, as the seat and cigar box banjo are identical to the other versions, entitled "Coontown Troubadour" featuring a single subject singing and playing.

Another postcard with the same title, "The Blackville Serenade," with completely different subjects is likely produced at a later date. Evidence from postmarked cards indicates that they were in circulation as early as 1936. They illustrate that the cigar box banjo is still in use, but they are probably more propaganda to uphold the Sambo stereotype than a genuine illustration of African-American lifestyle.

From a post-colonial interpretation, one could trace a musical path to the interaction between the colonizer and the colonized as well as the forced transplantation of African slaves into America. With each culture that came to America, a different set of traditions in musical instruments, communication, dance, song, and entertainment arrived. The give and take between the blending of cultures formed a ground fertile with the opportunity to grow a unique instrument and style. From the appropriation of African culture, language, song, and gesture, minstrelsy plays a dominant role in any post-colonial analysis of the history of the cigar box guitar. But this is not the distinction that I want to make with cigar box instruments. Beyond this paragraph, I will not seek to ruminate on the history from this perspective.

1920

The fact that the cigar box banjo is mentioned as a prop in a children's story printed in *The Ogden Standard Examiner*, August 14, 1920, provides evidence that the cigar box banjo and other cigar box instruments are being marginalized around this time. However, even though cigar box instruments are about to be largely ignored, they do take root with children as education objects started about this time.

UNCLE WIGGILY AND SAMMIE'S BANJO
Copyright, 1920, by McClure Newspaper
Syndicate
(By HOWARD R. GABIS.)

Uncle Wiggily started the phonograph in his hollow stump bungalow one day when, just after he had listened to a record where a piano played a sort of tag song with a tin horn, there came a knock on the door.

"Goodness me sake alive! I hope that isn't the Pipsisewah!" exclaimed Nurse Jane, who was also listening to the phonograph. "He is dreadfully fond of music—almost as fond as he is of your souse Uncle Wiggily, and-"

"Don't say that—you make me nervous!" exclaimed the rabbit gentleman, as he looked for another record. "Besides, I don't believe it's the Pip," he went on.

"No, it isn't," said Nurse Jane, looking out of the window, "it's Sammie Littletail, the rabbit boy, and he has a cigar box and a broom stick and a lot of things in his paws."

Hum suz dud!' laughed Uncle Wiggily. "I suppose he wants me to make him a hoop, as I did for Susie,"

"You can't make a rolling hoop out of a cigar box," spoke Nurse Jane.

"I don't know about that," answered Uncle Wiggily. "I never tried. But let Sammie in, and we'll see what he what he has to say."

Into the hollow stump bungalow came Sammie, the boy rabbit. "Oh, Uncle Wiggily!" Sammie exclaimed, trying to make his pink nose twinkle like his uncle's. "Will you please fix my banjo?"

"Fix your banjo? What's the matter with it?" the bunny gentleman wanted to know.

"Well, there's lots the matter," Sammie explained, "In the first place it isn't a banjo at all yet. I started to make one out of a cigar box, a broom handle and some pieces of string, but I guess I don't know how."

"What's a banjo?" asked Nurse Jane.

"Something to make tinkily-tinkle music on," Sammie said, "It's round, and has a handle on like a frying pan, and some strings and a head like a drum. And when you pick the strings they go 'tum-te-tum-tum,' and make nice music. You can make a banjo out of a cigar box and a stick for a handle and then you don't have to have a thing on it like a drum head," the rabbit boy went on, "only I don't know how."

"Well, let me see if I do," said Uncle Wiggily. So he stopped the phonograph which was trying to keep on playing by itself, and took the things Sammie had brought over.

There was an empty cigar box, a broom handle with the broom part sawed off, and some strings, and also some little pegs to wind the ends of the banjo strings on to tighten them, and make some play high music notes and others low music notes, like on a piano.

"Well, I guess I can make a banjo," said Uncle Wiggily and then he began. He fastened the broom handle on one end of the cigar box, cut some holes in the box to let out the sound, fastened on the strings and then tightened them on the pegs.

"Now I shall sing a song and play on Sammie's cigar box banjo," said Uncle Wiggily, crossing his legs and sitting down on the top step of the hollow stump bungalow.

The bunny gentleman picked the banjo strings, making a nice little music tune, and then he sang.

"Oh, ho Nurse Jane,
She's a nice muskrat!
She bakes minced pies.
And can trim a hat.

She keeps the bungalow
Nice and clean.
She's the best housekeeper
I have ever seen!"

"Oh, thank you Uncle Wiggily!" laughed Miss
Fuzzy Wuzzy "I didn't know you were such a.
good minstrel singer."

"Can you play another song on my banjo?" asked
Sammie much delighted.
"Yes," answered Uncle Wiggily and he sang and
played this one:

Sammy the rabbit,
Acts rather funny.
But you must remember
He is only a bunny.
"I sing and play
All day long,
But tell me how
You like this song."

And with that, before Sammie or Nurse Jane
could stop him. Uncle Wiggily suddenly stopped
singing, and, giving a hop, skip and jump off the
porch, he raised the bunny boy's banjo high in the
air and brought it smashing down on the head of
the bad Skeezicks, who, just then, started to hop
out from behind a big tree.

"There! Tell me how you like that song!" cried
Uncle Wiggily, as he threw the broken banjo after
the Skee. who ran away crying, "Wow! Wouch!
Scouch!"

"Oh, my nice banjo is all broken!" sadly said Sammie.

"Nevermind, I'll make you: another, promised Uncle Wiggily. "I happened to see the Skee sneaking up after my souse as I was singing and playing and I knew the only way to scare him was to do something surprising. And I did!"

"Yes," agreed Nurse Jane, "you certainly did!" But she found another cigar box and the bunny made a better banjo than before and Sammie learned to play it. And when the pepper caster comes up from having gone down in the salt cellar to set some powdered sugar, I'll tell you about Uncle Wiggily and Johnnie's shampoo.

1975

In Tom Keynton's *Homemade Musical Instruments*, Keynton describes a crude 4 string cigar box banjo with a piece of wood attached to the back of a cigar box which has a hole cut in the center to approximate a sound hole of a traditional guitar: "It may not be a musical instrument; much more likely a toy. But as a little boy I made my first banjo and it looked like this. My grandfather helped. It made good music, I thought, until the rubber bands broke."

Keynton's cigar box banjo sounded good until the rubber bands broke

The Cigar Box Ukulele

"The uke is... cool!"
-George Harrison

1917

Homemade Hawaiian Ukulele, as written by S. H. Samuels appears in the June issue of *Popular Mechanics*, and later in *The Boy Mechanic Book 3: 800 Things for a Boy to Do*. [See Historic Cigar Box Instrument Plans]

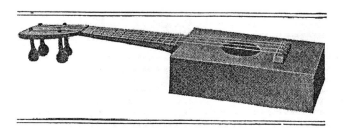

1922

In *The Charleston Daily Mail*, March 24, 1922. Charles Albert King published plans for a cigar box mandolin. This could possibly be the same Charles Albert King who published *Elements Of Woodwork* (1911) as well as other books on the topic. [See Historic Cigar Box Instrument Plans]

In this same year, the questionable account of Nunes and his claim of having invented the ukulele with the use of cigar box appears in several newspapers, among them *The Modesto Evening News*, August 2, 1922:

> Manuel Nunnes [sic], inventor of the ukulele, dies In Honolulu. He built the first ukulele out of a cigar box in 1879.

> The ukulele music, played by native Hawaiians, later swept our country as a craze, made popular by "The Bird of Paradise." This music is a hash of old-time camp-meeting songs taken across the Pacific by missionaries.

> Nunnes [sic] was a powerful man, His invention swayed the emotions of millions. Too bad we can't set common sense to music. May be we could. No one ever tried it. With economics in ragtime form, even statistics would be interesting.

While it is interesting to think that Nunes first made a ukulele from a cigar box, there is no other evidence than this obituary to support it. The article is likely a national wire story, as the death of Nunes was published in newspapers across the United States. Notices of his death in the two major Honolulu papers during that time credit Nunes with the invention of the instrument; they say nothing about the use of cigar boxes. [See Sam Kamaka Jr.]

Later in this same year, the October 13 edition of *Logansport Pharos-Tribune*, New York Day by Day with O.O. McIntyre reports

> Bobby Edwards, the cigar box ukulele troubadour of Greenwich Village, is again appearing on the stage. This season he yodels: I sing of Greenwich Village and its amateur distillage. Bobby is one of the quaint character of Bohomia who clings persistently to village life. He is the graduate of a famous college and a fellow of great erudition. Yet he is happiest when surrounded by his cronies at a coffee shop table, singing and playing his uke.

First appearing in the *Aunt Elsie Magazine Of The Oakland Tribune*, October 8, 1922, and then again (with some corrections in spelling) in *The Janesville Daily Gazette*, January 25, 1923, Lewis Allen Brown wrote the plans for a cigar box ukulele in Adventure Trails Blazed For You: [See Historic Cigar Box Instrument Plans]

This "Our Gang" character is child actor Allen "Farina" Hoskins who was one of the characters in the 1922 silent era. Born Allen Clayton Hoskins August 9, 1920, he was the character of Farina in the "Our Gang" short films from 1922 to 1931. Farina was intended to be the typical Pickaninny in the tradition of the character Topsy from Uncle Tom's Cabin. Later on, as his character became one of the better known ones, Allen developed the character in his own special style apart from the stereotype he was original cast as. He got the name "Farina" from a type of cereal. While acting in "Our Gang," Farina became one of its most popular characters. Later on in his last contract with the Hal Roach Studio he was making $250 a week, more than any other child star at that time. Farina left the series in

1931 at the age of eleven and was replaced by Matthew "Stymie" Beard. [http://www.findagrave.com]

Farina of Our Gang Playing as One-Man Band in Promo Picture

ca. 1926

In 1977 *Hecho en Tejas* was published and featured a section on Miguel Acosta, a fourth generation stringed instrument maker. While his is not a particularly stunning contribution to the history here, it does place a cigar box ukulele in the timeline around 1926. According to James C. McNutt:

> Miguel Acosta, born in 1918, belongs to a family which for four generations has been making, repairing, and selling stringed instruments... Miguel began making instruments at age eight, combining an old ukelele neck with a Finck cigar box.

These underwhelming one-line statements about people getting started with cigar box instruments are not uncommon. Many examples are stated elsewhere in the timeline.

1931

In October 1931, in *Comfort Magazine*, Charles Albert King published a similar set of plans for a Cigar Box Uke to his 1922 plans for a cigar box mandolin. [See Historic Cigar Box Instrument Plans]

1936

In the January 31, 1936 edition of the *Olean Times-Herald* (and also in the *Logansport Pharos-Tribune*), O.O. McIntyre writes in the New York Day by Day column,

> Hype Igoe is likely the dean of active sports writers in Manhattan -- and high among top notchers. He draws as robustly as he writes. Through the years his boxing predictions have been amazingly accurate -- Although his articles show no letup in enthusiasm, life has never been

quite the same since the passing of Tad. They were reared south of the slot in San Francisco, began their careers and trekked East together. Tad laughed himself out of a thousand trains to Great Neck. Igoe sang to the thrum of his cigar box ukulele in the old Battling Nelson Grill of Jack's.

2004

The Hawaii Post issued, on August 23rd 2004, a stamp booklet celebrating the 125th Anniversary of the Ukulele. The booklet included 2 panes containing 2 x $5 and 2 x $8 stamps. The white card stock front cover shows 3 different ukuleles: The pineapple ukulele, a standard ukulele, and a cigar box ukulele.

The Cigar Box Guitar

*"There is no right way to do
the wrong thing."*
- Unknown

Throughout the history of cigar box guitars and its relatives, there are numerous one-line mentions of people making cigar box instruments. Often in these accounts, a parent or relative will make such a thing for a child to play with either for entertainment, as a toy, or as a legitimate noise maker. In some cases, the one-line reference gives a few details of the box used and the source of the string – be it an electrical wire from a car or a strand of wire pulled from a window screen. The creativity of these individuals proves that there is more than one way to create these makeshift instruments. Is it the wrong way to make a playable instrument? It is, perhaps, if examined from the point of view of traditional instrument making. However, through my own curiosity about these crude instruments, I have discovered that cigar box instruments have a tradition unique to themselves, and because of that, they are equally as valid an instrument as their traditional counterparts.

Based on my own research and the artifacts I have collected in the cigar box guitar museum, untold numbers of cigar box instruments have been crafted and cherished for decades; while makers are legion, their names are unknown. Beyond the fact that we know the instruments have been made, the maker, their intent, and their inspiration remain a mystery. Only the artifact of the instrument itself remains. In a few exceptional cases, the entire provenance of an instrument, from its maker to its player – who may or may not be the same person – and other external events surrounding the instrument itself are known.

What about the earliest cigar box guitar, if there is such a thing? Searching through the contents of this history, the first sign of the "cigar box guitar" in that exact wording is actually in the form of the cigar box ukulele. Strangely enough, the first mention of a cigar box guitar comes from a set of ukulele plans by S. H. Samuels that were published in 1917 in *Popular Mechanics*. Is it fair to call a cigar box ukulele a cigar box guitar? Well, actually yes, if we consult a definitive resource, the Oxford English Dictionary. The OED defines a ukulele as – a small Hawaiian four-string guitar. Well, what about the other instruments defined in the OED as being variants of the lute and guitar?

Any 4-stringed cigar box banjo, as long as it is missing the short string and tuning peg half-way up the neck, could equally qualify as a cigar box guitar. In fact, 4-stringed banjos in the shape of a guitar are called tenor guitars. So, in that case, another search through this history shows a cigar box guitar in banjo form dating back as far as 1891 in the "C.T. Southern Pickaninny Scenes" postcards that feature at least 5 different images of 4 string cigar box instruments being played.

1917

The first confirmed mention of a "cigar box guitar" comes from S. H. Samuels plans of how to build a cigar box *ukulele* in the June issue of *Popular Mechanics* which states, "The one-string banjo, the cigar box guitar, and similar vaudeville favorites are giving way to the tantalizing ukulele." [See Historic Cigar Box Instrument Plans]

1923

In 1923, Doc Watson is born and he will eventually be the father of country music by establishing the first hillbilly band. According to the PBS *Austin City Limits* program guide:

Watson was born in Stoney Fork, N.C., in 1923. The area is recognized as one of the most productive regions in the United States for "homemade music." The original "banjoman," Frank Proffitt, hailed from nearby Beech Mountain. The first country string band, The Hill Billies (from which the term came), was organized only a few miles from Watson's home.

Although the first instrument that he learned to play was the harmonica, it didn't take Watson long to become interested in the guitar.

"I really didn't start learning a little guitar until I was three," Watson said. "I remember my daddy made me a little *bajo* [a Spanish bass] out of a hickory sapling sometime before that, but the guitar didn't really interest me until a little later. Once I got interested, it stayed with me though."

Doc Watson's homemade bajo would have likely been made around 1926 given the information in the PBS guide.

1924

The June issue of *Practical Electrics* (Vol 3 No 8) published plans for the "Hot Wire Guitar." Although it is not a proper electric guitar as an instrument, it is the first indication of electronics being used on a guitar, and could be considered the first electric guitar ever made. It is also, apparently, an early mention of a cigar box guitar, despite the fact that it is impractical.

> An interesting musical instrument of electrical operation can be constructed out of a cigar box and a few parts similar to those used on the ordinary string musical instruments. The illustration gives an idea of how the instrument is constructed.

> The one shown has but one steel string. The tension of this string is increased until it will vibrate at the highest musical not desired. The string is fastened to binding posts at each end, and a battery and rheostat are connected to the binding posts. As the current through the string, it heats the string, which expands, the tension decreases and the note is lowered.

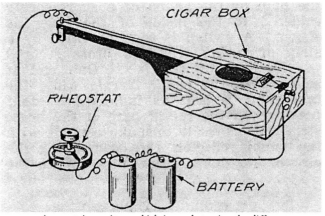

A one-string guitar, which is made to give the different notes of the musical scale by being heated more or less by passing an electric current through the wire.

By means of the rheostat the amount of current passing through the string is steadily controlled and hence any musical note desired can be obtained. By controlling the rheostat with one hand and picking the string with the other, music similar to that obtained from a Hawaiian guitar can be produced after a little practice. If desired, two ore more string may be employed, with a rheostat for each string.

1925

The first mention of a functional six-string cigar box guitar comes from "The Old City Of Marseilles" in *Gambrinus and Other Stories* by Aleksandr Ivanovich Kuprin, published 1925, which is consistent with the fact that he moved and lived in Paris from 1919 to 1937. Kuprin described this colorful scene:

ONE MAN'S TRASH

In his hands he carries an odd musical instrument. It consists of an ordinary cigar box, upon which are still preserved the black, oval trade-marks, Colorado. A round opening has been sawn in the lid. A small, narrow board, crudely glued on to the box, serves as its neck. There are homemade keys and six fine strings.

This man does not exchange greetings with any one, and does not even seem to see anybody. He calmly squats down near the counter; then he lies down along its length, upon the bare floor, face upward. For a few seconds he tunes his amazing instrument, then loudly calls out, in the jargon of the south, the name of some popular national song, and, still lying down, commences to play.

I am very fond of the guitar, that tender, chanting, expressive instrument, and I have frequent occasion to hear artists who have the mastery of virtuosos on this instrument, up to celebrities, known to all Russia. But still, up to this incident, I could never imagine that a piece of wood with strings and ten human digits could create such full and harmonious singing music. The cigar box of this curious old man sang with silvern sounds, just like a distant, splendid choir, composed of children, women, or angels.

1930

Tommy Lee "Legs" Thompson in an interview originally published in *Blues Unlimited* No. 66 states:

I was born down here in 1915. I would say I was somewhere about 15 when I started to playing.

The Cigar Box Guitar

Made me a guitar. Taken me a cigar box and a guitar neck and I played several parties with it. I worked places. I could play behind most anybody when I was working and recording.

1936

As told in *Guitar Player* in 1976, Carl Perkins (1932 – 1998) love for the guitar began at age four, when his father built his first one from a cigar box, a broomstick, and bailing wire.

1937

James Aswell writes in *The Oshkosh Northwestern,* September 8, 1937, and also in *The Hammond Times* on the same day (with a few typos introduced as well):

My New York

The obsession with weird and improvised musical instruments is pervading this neck of the woods, with particular appeal for the professional musicians. The range of instrumental variety is almost unlimited—the noseophone, the comb-and-tissuepaper, the musical saw, the cigarbox guitar, only serve to give an idea.

Look at the face of one of the operators of these screwy instruments while he plays. A beatific look creeps into his eyes and spreads all over his face as he blows convulsively or scrapes assiduously.

A master of the cigar box, one stringed instrument is Phil Baker, who otherwise is an expert on the accordion. Phil can get more music out of the one-stringed instrument than many musicians get out of a whole violin section of the New York Philharmonic. He always has a piece of catgut in his pocket, for wherever he goes he can always pick up a cigar box. In a few seconds he rigs a fret board on the cigar box, attaches the string from one end to the other and starts his music going.

1938

The book *Blow for a Landing* by Ben Lucien Burman is first published in 1938. There is a connection to W.C. Handy's story in that Willow Joe's mother and W.C. Handy's mother both referred to the guitar as being "the worst kind of sin." And even later in both of their lives there is the strong hint of a reluctant acceptance to their becoming a musician.

> Lazy and good-natured, he [Willow Joe] leaves most of the productive work to his brother Opal while he loafs along the wharves and river banks with his cigar-box guitar and a set of musical jugs.

In his autobiography, W.C. Handy remembers his first guitar. Unlike Willow Joe who fashioned one out of a cigar box, Handy worked odd jobs and saved his money to purchase a guitar from a local department store. Because of the desire to buy this guitar, he found the means to purchase one. He took pride in the ownership while he owned it. Regrettably, his mother forced him to return the guitar and exchange it for an encyclopedia. However, he, for a short time, felt a great pride in that first guitar. He worked for it. He *owned* it.

The Cigar Box Guitar

The April 29, 1938 edition of the *San Antonio Light*
provides a review of *Blow for a Landing* featured in the
"Rivers and Dictators" column of Edwin C. Hill.

> He has an ear as sensitive and accurate as that of
> any current writing man. In the tale of Willow Joe
> Penny, with his cigar box guitar and his musical
> Jugs, and the struggle of Willow Joe and his family
> against the elemental force of the river, he
> achieves a dramatization of a friendly little man
> against dark and stark fate which is, quite
> ingenuously, in the classic Greek tradition. I found
> the book fascinating reading, not only as a throw-
> back to the vast, brooding America which we used
> to think we knew, but as an escape from the
> psycho-analytical jungles through which some of
> our leading literati have been leading us.
> Incidentally, there is no better master of the idiom
> of the river clans than Mr. Burman.

1944

Joe Barry – Swamp Pop legend makes a cigar box guitar
at the age of five. According to *Swamp Pop Cajun and
Creole Rhythm and Blues* by Shane K. Bernard:

> Born Joseph Barrios on July 12, 1939, in Cut Off
> – a small bayou town in Laforche Parish, in
> eastern Acadiana – he grew up in a poor Cajun
> family... his father possessed an interest in music
> (he played the harmonica and Jew's harp), as did
> many of Barry's relatives.
>
> Barry first expressed an interest in music around
> age five, when he fashioned a makeshift guitar
> from a cigar box and a wire from a screen door. A

123

brother soon presented him with a neglected guitar, on which Barry taught himself to play (in about two days, he says). His parents shortly bought him a new Stella brand guitar...

1976

The December 1976 issue of *Guitar Player* magazine featured Michael Lydon's article "A Great American Tradition, The Cigar Box Guitar," which begins with a quote from Carl Perkins. [See Historic Cigar Box Instrument Plans]

1982

Kurt Loder writes on the classic blues life of Lightnin' Hopkins in *Rolling Stone*, issue number 365:

His was a classic blues life, which is to say it was courageous in a fundamental way. Sam Hopkins was born March 15th, 1912, in Centerville, Texas, a small farm town north of Houston. His father, Abe, who died when Sam was still a baby, was a musician, and so were Sam's sister and four brothers. He was encouraged by his mother to play the organ at the family's home church services, but his first real musical influence was his guitar-playing brother, John Henry, later a noted bluesman himself. At age eight, Sam built his own guitar, cutting a hole in a cigar box, nailing on a plank for the neck and stringing the thing with chicken wire.

He took his guitar to a Baptist picnic in nearby Buffalo on Sunday afternoon in the summer of

1920, and there encountered his second major influence – the church association had hired the great Blind Lemmon Jefferson to sing at the picnic. Sam stole up to the platform where Jefferson was performing and attempted to play along "I was so little and low, they couldn't see me," he later recalled. Jefferson, annoyed by Hopkins' noodling, stopped short and shouted: "Boy, you got to play it *right.*" Lesson number one.

1994

A brief mention of a cigar box guitar on display is mentioned in the June 7, 1994 edition of *The Daily Herald of Tyrone PA*:

EXHIBIT TRACES CHANGES IN THE AMERICAN GUITAR

Popular music owes a debt to this most humble of stringed instruments and you need only head to the National Museum of American History to pay your respects. A new exhibit, "Guitars in American Popular Music," opens today and showcases more than a dozen of the guitars in the collection. The exhibit illustrates the changes that saw the guitar to its present state and charts the past 100 years of America's love affair with the instrument. There are folk, acoustic and electric guitars. There is a resonator guitar, a cigar box guitar, a plastic guitar and a double necked harp-guitar.

Exhibit curator Bill Yardley called the guitar "one of those rare trends that caught on and stuck." "The guitar was embraced by popular culture," he said. "It struck a common chord in this country. And in the end ... these things are still here in our culture."

1998

365 More Simple Science Experiments With Everyday Objects published "plans" for a cigar box guitar made from rubber bands on an empty box. While I disagree with calling such a creation a guitar, the number of times this noise maker is suggested in the timeline deserves mentioning.

Rubber bands make for calling this a guitar quite a stretch

Vaudeville

*"Failure   is   the   only
opportunity to begin again
more intelligently."*
                -Henry Ford

Cigar box instruments were a mainstay in the "low art" world of vaudeville. Cigar box instruments were used for comedic effect or for showing true musical prowess to demonstrate that fine music could be played on a primitive contraption. Performances of this type were very often well-received by the audience

The history of vaudeville provides a rare opportunity to look back into the past at a time when the cigar box violin or fiddle was a common sight. It is my speculation that what we read about these contraptions in vaudeville shows is just the tip of the iceberg. Vaudeville had a reputation of using ethnic and racial stereotypes as the subject matter for many of its acts, including, most prominently, black face minstrelsy. These acts, while completely inappropriate for a modern audience, were commonplace in the days of vaudeville. Also, the acts were often based on genuine people, exaggerated for the purpose of entertainment on stage. So, my speculation about vaudeville being only the tip of the iceberg comes from this unsettling knowledge that these performers on the stage were based on performances of genuine people playing these makeshift instruments. Sadly, the inspiration for what was seen on the stage was rarely recorded.

There are exceptions, however, but it is not through vaudeville's lens that we see these real-life examples. It is from the work of people like Alan Lomax who went into the segregated South of the Mississippi Delta to make field recordings of the early works of blues musicians, to interview them about their music, and about their early days on the way to becoming a musician that we gain a true perspective of how and why the cigar box instruments were made.

1905

An image from a postcard dated April 23, 1905 shows musician Leo Wildon, who, based on his dress, would qualify as a prominently featured vaudeville act. He is pictured playing a Stroh violin, another mechanical oddity essentially combining a violin and phonograph for amplification. Two cigar box violins are visible behind Leo, to the right.

Leo Wildon Playing a Stroh Violin

1910

Whether used as a gimmick or as a serious instrument, in the hands of the right player, a cigar box violin could produce sweet music. The August 7, 1910 edition of the

San Antonio Light and Gazette published an account about such music at the Hot Wells Hotel:

HOT WELLS OPEN AIR CAFE

This has become the fixed popular summer garden. With an entire change of vocal offerings and an entirely new orchestra the musical program is now complete. P. Persia's famous orchestra is drawing new and larger attendances every evening. Mr. Persia, who plays Schubert's Serenade and other classical pieces on his cigar box violin, is a master of note. The violin is made of a common cigar box and has only one string. The accuracy and sweetness of his notes on such a crude instrument is simply a marvel. Mr. Persia himself made the "cigar box violin" and his ability in playing such classical pieces on the one string is a rare treat.

1911

Cigar box fiddles in vaudeville continue to delight audiences as evidenced from the *San Antonio Light*, February 18, 1911:

THE ROYAL

A piece of ordinary wire, strung on a broom handle, fingered with an ordinary cigar box and played by a fiddle bow is not calculated to make good music as a rule. But Fred El[h]ott, one of the acts on the Royal bill, dually, makes the sweetest of music out of the odd combination. It is not musical act, however, just a comedy skit, the broom fiddle serving as a hot finish. The big crowds last night insisted on hearing more of the broom fiddle music, but owing to the fast schedule of Sunday night they were forced to be content without it.

1912

The November 20, 1912 edition of *The La Crosse Tribune* publishes under the headline of PRIMA DONNA IS VODVIL FEATURE, about a gifted one-string cigar box violin player.

> "Karl," the man with the one string cigar box fiddle, is another character on this last half week's bill familiar to local people. "Karl" first appeared in La Crosse when he was a traveling salesman, and took his fiddle on at the old Bijou on amateur night. The tones he manages to draw from the dilapidated instrument are wonderful. It is something between a 'cello and a violin in tone, and under his expert fingers whistles like a Bird or talks like a woman. Classic and ragtime are all in his repertoire.

From *The Syracuse Herald*, February 28, 1912, an unusual set of plans are printed to make a cigar box zither. [See Historic Cigar Box Instrument Plans]

1914

The January 2, 1914 edition of *The La Crosse Tribune* published a rave review about the line up at another vaudeville show. In this case, Musical Fletcher is placed on the bill as the most entertaining act of the show.

ONE MAN'S TRASH

SPLENDID BILL AT THE MAJESTIC
THEATRE

Manager Koppelberger's New Year Greetings to
City Arrive in Shape of Dandy Show...
Musical Fletcher is an orchestra in himself. He
succeeds in getting much music out of a cigar box
fiddle and an old watering can which he
transforms into a flute. His best stunt is with eight
beer bottles, each containing a different amount of
water so that on striking they sound an entire
octave. He renders many popular songs on this
improvised instrument.

An act's placement on the bill, according to the
American Masters Production *Vaudeville*, determined
how successful they were and how good the act was. To
play first was forgettable. The opening act was typically
silent and easily ignored; vaudevillians didn't want to
open the show. Animals opened too, often over human
objections. Appearing second on the bill wasn't much
better. The second act was usually a singing-sister act.
The third spot were often short, one-act plays
performed by legitimate actors. As told by vaudevillians,
the plays were really not all that good, and audiences
sometimes became restless. The following acts woke up
the audience, though. Right before intermission were
near-headliners, rising stars or falling stars. The big acts
played right after intermission – big bands, big
production numbers, or big "nut acts" like Jimmy
Durand. The most coveted spot on the bill was next-to-
last. If an act was placed there, it meant that they were a
star, or at least the best on the bill. The closing spot was
called "playing to the haircuts" because that's what they
saw going up the aisle, as people left before the show
was officially over. To drive audiences away, to make

room for the next audience, managers would *purposely* book bad acts for closing.

Even with rave review after rave review found in newspapers on vaudeville entertainment, this curious review in the June 15, 1914 edition of the *Stephens Point Daily Journal* gives a glimpse of the demise of vaudeville. As motion pictures came into fashion, live entertainment from vaudeville eventually became a much too expensive option: performers had to be paid and travel expenses covered. Once vaudeville performances were committed to film, the acts performed live lost their appeal, for the motion picture of the original act could be sent cheaply and allowed a filmed performance of the same act again and again.

VAUDEVILLE ATTRACTION AT GRAND SATURDAY AND SUNDAY

The acts are "big city" bills, produced by the Western Vaudeville Managers' association, and they satisfied. Mack and Soheftels, comedy singers and talkers, are clever and their strong, clear voices blend together perfectly. Karl, "The Wizard of the one string", brings forth remarkable tones from his cigar box "fiddle" and the audience couldn't help becoming good natured while he entertained them musically and with his rapid fire talking. Gangler's dogs almost talked; in fact they did talk in their own way. They went through their little "playlet" without a falter and required very little prompting from their master. Three reels of movies completed the show and it was well worth the money.

ONE MAN'S TRASH

1918

In the context of this article from the *Chester Times* on April 18, 1918, this ingenious performer is a treat, unless compared to moving pictures, and his playing is welcome to young boys who laugh to hear the sounds of the cigar box fiddle.

AN INGENIOUS PERFORMER

A real treat, outside of moving pictures, was given yesterday by Frank Monteiro, of the Empire Engineer's Company, who went through, the town playing operatic airs on a fiddle, made out of a cigar box.

Monterio is a Portuguese – a good citizen, who has lived here for the past five years, and along the way he played "Lucia" and other popular operettas on a makeshift violin, made out of an ordinary cigar box. There were three strings to it. The bow, he whittled out of a piece of wood, as he stood in front of his auditors and then with a touch of an artist he played on the old cigar box some of the finest operatic airs and popular songs of the day.

Operas on an old cigar box, made the Boys all laugh and there was a cheerful handout.

I am not sure what to make of this article printed on May 20, 1918, in the *Chester Times*. The popularity of the vaudeville shows continue to wane, but the subject matter that one might expect to see in such a venue is relegated in this instance to young children – featuring a blackface act, as well as a one string fiddle:

Vaudeville

MANY MEETINGS TODAY

This evening at the Chester Playhouse, Seventh street bridge, the Baldwin Locomotive Works workers will stage an all-star show which promises to surpass anything of the sort ever attempted by local talent. The program was arranged by C. C. Elms, assistant superintendent of the Baldwin plant.

Among the high spots on the program will be an Irish sketch by Joe and John O'Donnell, a blackface act in which Joe Hawley will appear, Bill Robinson will show how much real music can be gotten out of a one string fiddle made up from an ax handle and a cigar box, the Baldwin Glee Club of 24 singers will offer for your approval, ladies' and gentlemen, a choice selection of war songs and other popular hits. The director of the club is John Kimball. The Baldwin Locomotive works will play a strictly up-to-date collection of classic and popular music, under the leadership of George Black. C. H. Eckstein will direct an unusually fine orchestra. The "Haunted House" will afford a number of the boys an opportunity to show their ability as comedians.

1920

The world surrounding the cigar box violin is moving on, finding a new home in the hands of children for their musical education and in the hands of the soldiers of World War I. Yet as reported in *The Olean Evening Herald*, September 28, 1920, vaudeville still holds to its tried-and-true acts of black face comedians and novelty instruments made from cigar boxes.

135

ONE MAN'S TRASH

In the Theatres
PALACE

When it comes to real out and out comedy that makes you laugh in spite of yourself, Salle and Rouble, who are appearing as one of the feature vaudeville acts at the Palace theatre for the first half of this week "win the brown derby." Their act is styled "eccentric comedy" and it is all of that and then some. The two young men, one working straight and the other in character, offer an entire new line of chatter that has the audience by storm the minute they appear on the stage.

Lew Rice, a black face comedian, presents a comedy singing and talking novelty which is well received. Not the least feature of his act is the playing of a "one string fiddle" cleverly constructed out of a cigar box. Rice really gets a remarkable tone out of his improvised instrument and plays it with more expression than many so called artists get out of a regular violin.

1924

In 1924, as an increasingly more common association is made between cigar box instruments and comedy acts, the rave reviews of cigar box violins in vaudeville theaters become fewer and farther between as evidenced in February 20, 1924, *The Galveston Daily News*.

TALENTED RUSSIANS FEATURE OFFERING AT GRAND OPERA HOUSE.

Dave Roth, a versatile comic, who played the piano, danced and attempted singing after [in] a nasal fashion, got away with a good many hands and his sensational dummy dancing stunt at the end left the audience guessing whether he had a dummy or a real girl for a partner, His movie piano player impersonation was good, he could handle his feet well and his one-string cigar box "violin" was an oddity that produced real music in his hands.

1929

As Mordecai M. Kaplan observed in his journals after going to a vaudeville show on May 30, 1929, his reaction to the show is a mixture of admiration and near pity.

Some of the vaudeville artists appear to me to be super-men and women. They represent to me manifestations of human power, power highly organized and developed to the point of utmost skill. There was a young fellow, for example, who mimicked various dialects, sang, danced and played on a one string violin improvised out of a cigar box. I imagine that he too is often bored by the monotony of the few tricks which he has to perform, but seeing and hearing him as I do for the first time, I look upon him as a demi-god.

Could it be that Kaplan admired these artists, equating them to supermen and superwomen, because of their ability to continue to perform the same monotonous routines show after show? Kaplan even wonders about the monotony of improvisation on a one string cigar box violin.

Movies & Radio

*"If vaudeville had died,
television was the box they
put it in."*
        - Larry Gelbart

Robert Mott, in his first hand account captured in *Radio Sound Effects*, recalls how radio sound effects received tremendous help from the failing burlesque houses and vaudeville theaters, especially from the techniques and talents of the trap drummers. In addition to musical responsibilities, a trap drummer was expected to supply sound effects for the various acts. To accommodate the requests made by performers the drummers had a huge assortment of props for "whiz-bangs" or the odorous "BEE OHH" horn.

Used primarily in comedy, the Boing Box, as Mott describes it, consisted of a guitar G string attached to a turntable pickup head that was connected to a speaker. By plucking the string and squeezing the handle it produced a comedic "boing" sound. This cousin of the cigar box guitar is probably the most recognizable and most often heard example of any cigar box instrument.

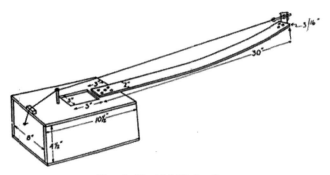

Turnbull's 1951 Boing Box

1921 - Lee Moran

From 1915-1920, Moran was one half of a popular comedy team in silent shorts. The lanky, long-faced vaudevillian began working in film in 1909 at Nestor Studios. While appearing in one- and two-reel comedies for producer Al Christie in 1915, Moran was teamed with Earle Lyons.

Forsaking pure slapstick in favor of situational humor, the Lyons-Moran comedies were extremely successful; their winning streak was interrupted only when Lyons and Moran decided to go their separate ways in 1920. After the breakup, Moran starred and directed in such feature-length endeavors as "La La Lucille" (1920), then signed on as producer, director, writer, and actor with the newly formed Arrow Studios. When talkies came in, Moran concentrated exclusively on acting, working as a supporting player until his retirement in 1936.

1927

Speaking to the importance of instruments to the new medium of radio, J.T.W. Martin writes in *The Times*,

March 3, 1927; this article also appeared in the *San Antonio Express*, March 27, 1927.

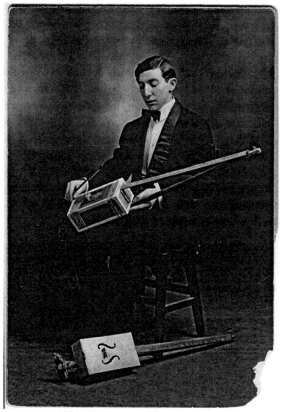

Vaudevillian Lee Moran in 1921

REJUVENATING MUSICAL INSTRUMENTS

If spring house cleaning this year brings to light any odd-looking musical instruments, don't relegate them to the trash heap without first taking them to the nearest broadcasting studio and having them tested over the air. Broadcasting has dragged plenty of almost forgotten instruments into prominence, and it has helped to popularize a host of new ones. And the process will undoubtedly continue just as long as musical tools which register through the microphone with new dualities of tone can be discovered or created.

The members of the program departments of the National Broadcasting company [sic], who are responsible for the booking of artists who appear over the air from stations WEAF and WJZ of New York, WRC of Washington and KFKX of Hastings Neb, have become immune to outlandish names for musical instruments. No longer can a performer create a stir by declaring emphatically that he is a past master of the bathyphon or a wizard with the cheng.

Push button sound effects, mechanical drum, harmonica, cigar box ukulele, and foot operated guitar made a lot of noise for this CBS microphone

Instead, they ask him to play it before a microphone in the studio, so that they may hear it in a loud speaker and decide whether or not it is suitable for broadcasting. The program builders have even ceased to be amused when the artist produces from his pocket an instrument bearing a strange, seven-syllabled name, or when he states that a truck is outside bearing an implement whose name can be recorded in three letters.

Many of the weirdly named instruments are old ones. Others have just come on the market, but these are usually adaptations or mechanical variations of ancient musical tools. Some of them proved unsuited to broadcasting, but plenty of them have made established places for themselves in the ranks of instruments well suited to microphone work. At any rate, the program builders are always open minded, they refuse to pass judgment until the mike has had its say.

Before the advent of broadcasting few people had heard of the celeste, although it had always been a part of every full symphony orchestra. The instrument consists of a number of steel plates which are played by being struck with small hammers, a description which sounds considerably less melodious than the sweet tones which the celeste produces in broadcasting. Today, the instrument is being used by many popular orchestras in their concerts over the air.

The xylophone, the marimba and the cymbalum, all implements similar in construction to the celeste, have also been brought to fame largely by radio, and the vibraphone, which produces its tones from metal tubes rather than from strings or discs, has been designed especially for broadcasting purposes.

The microphone made musical saws and cigar box fiddles
practical for radio use

Almost anything can be played these days. Witness the sweet, swinging tones of a saw when struck with a padded hammer and bent to produce various notes. The cigar-box banjo and the "one-string fiddle," made from a cigar box and a broomstick, in the hands of experienced players, produce real music of a startlingly different character when heard over the air.

Other instruments which have proved excellent broadcasters are legion. They include the zither, a form of Irish harp once very popular but little heard of late, until broadcasting came into its own. The dulcimer and the harpsichord, forerunners of the modern piano, are making new musical reputations, thanks to the microphone. Even the Jew's harp is gathering laurels for itself.

Thee are others, of course—hundreds of them, probably. And hardly a week goes by that some new instrument is not offered to the National Broadcasting company [sic] program departments for testing. Still, the process goes on. New instruments are brought to light or manufactured, and some of them which suit microphone requirements become famous through broadcasting.

1929

Mickey Mouse, in "Mickey's Follies," one of many of the early Walt Disney cartoons which ran before the main feature in theaters, appeared in a band with Mickey on the piano and a cat playing a one-string cigar box fiddle in a very familiar vaudevillian style.

*Cat plays one-string fiddle and Mickey Mouse accompanies on piano
(Mickey Mouse image Copyright © Disney Enterprises, Inc)*

1930

Often the cartoons showed before the features were as popular as the feature itself. Movie goers that saw this poster knew that Mickey Mouse would be shown before the main feature.

Around this same year (ca. 1927 to 1931), the first known recording of a cigar box guitar is credited to Beans Hambone. According to the liner notes in the compilation CD *Good For What Ails You: Music of the Medicine Shows 1926-1937:*

Movie poster promises that Mickey Mouse will be shown here today
(Mickey Mouse image Copyright © Disney Enterprises, Inc)

According to the legendary record collector, Pete Whelan, James Albert, a.k.a. "Beans Hambone" and his partner El Morrow were musicians from North Carolina. They recorded just two songs for the Victor Record Company, "Beans" and "Tippin' Out." Beans Hambone provided the main vocals and plays what is thought to be a cigar box banjo [because of the out of tune notes that he plays]. El Morrow backs Beans up on a standard guitar.

147

1936

A few vaudeville performers were successful in making the transition to the silver screen. Among them, W.C. Fields, who starred in "Poppy" according to the August 8, 1936 edition of the *Oakland Tribune.*

> W. C. Fields In "Poppy" and "One Rainy Afternoon," with Frances Lederer and Ida Lupino, are the attractions starting at the Alameda tomorrow. Gettysburg, Waterloo, Actium, Jutland, great battles these, but they are said to be mere skirmishes beside Fields' fight to a finish with shirt front, croquet mallet, suspender strap and cigar box fiddle.

W. C. Fields in "Poppy" with one-string cigar box fiddle

These are some of the matters with which "Poppy" deals. Fields captures his audience this time in the role of a gentleman who lives by his wits, taking cash, food and drink when and where he may.

And for acts not seen on the screen, there was always the increasingly popular form of entertainment in the radio, as mentioned here in the *Winnipeg Free Press*, January 19, 1935:

SUNDAY YOU WILL HEAR...

...A violin solo played on a cigar box fiddle will be the high-light of the House by the Side of the road programme at 4.30 p.m. (KFYR). 'Traumerie' will be the selection.

1951

Plans for a Boing Box are published in *Radio and Television Sound Effects* by Robert B. Turnbull. [See Historic Cigar Box Instrument Plans]

Trench Art

"The aim of art is to represent not the outward appearance of things, but their inward significance."
- Aristotle

With the onset of World War I in 1914, cigar box instruments found a new home in the hands of soldiers as what would become eventually known as trench art.

Home Sweet Home, Again

1916

Flight Lieutenant E. L. Ford of the Royal Naval Air Service was the illustrator for *Practical Flying Complete Course of Flying Instructions* by Flight Commander W. G. McMinnies, Royal Navy, published in 1918.

Ford's one-string jap fiddle, illustrated text, and custom case

While in command of the Advanced Aerodromes in the Near East in 1916, Ford constructed this one-string Japanese fiddle from plane parts, cigar box, catgut from the medical officer, and wire. Hair from a horse's tail was fixed to the bow with sealing wax. The case for the cigar box fiddle was made by the mechanics, complete with inner cover; the case, in fact, appears to be better made than the instrument!

1918

According to the *Fitchburg Daily Sentinel*, April 24, 1918:

BENEFIT DANCE FOR ARMY BAND

The Camp Devens depot brigade band, which delighted Fitchburg people on Patriots day by playing for the Putnam celebration and also at a patriotic meeting at the armory, will conduct a concert and dance in city hall, May 9, for the benefit of the band and the 28th company of the depot brigade. There will be at least 15 musicians in the orchestra, which will play for dancing. The novelty entertainment which will be presented in connection with the dance will be provided by Bernard Satz, Fred Hannon and "Dotty" O'Connor, singers and musicians.

Mr. Satz has been on the Keith circuit and also appeared at the Bijou theater a few years ago. He is one of the first to play the trench fiddle, a single string on a cigar box, and is a good singer and clever entertainer. Mr. O'Connor has been heard in this section several times and needs no comment. He was with the Pathe Motion Picture Co. and has had extensive stage and screen experience.

The depot brigade band occupies a peculiar position. It is the only band not recognized by the war department. Hence it had to be satisfied with whatever instruments it could procure. It managed to land a number of brass instruments and those who heard it Patriots day can easily realize that with the latest and most modern instruments the band would compare with any at the camp. The orchestra will be under the direction of Sergt. William Schafer, who was with Sousa's band until he left to lead the depot brigade band for Uncle Sam.

ONE MAN'S TRASH

1919

In 1919, the Library of Congress acquired Edwin Forbes' original works through a gift from John Pierpont Morgan. The works included about 300 drawings as well as 43 etched plates and the original impressions used in *Life Studies of the Great Army.*

Meanwhile, the need for musical instruments in the lives of the soldiers that served in World War I, led, in some cases, to new careers. In this account printed in the *Middletown Daily Times-Express,* September 2, 1919, the creation of Private Jack Tender's cigar box fiddle led to greater things after the war.

CIGAR BOX FIDDLER BECAMES OVERSEAS STAR

Aided and abetted by the Y. M. C. A., Private Jack Tender of Passaic. N. J. made his own ragtime violin while in Base Hospital 120 before the armistice and as a result found himself doing big time on the A. E. F. circuit after the war was over.

It came about on account of the shortage of violins in France and because the Y. M. C. A. at 120 had raked the country unsuccessfully for the fiddle that Private Tender wanted more than anything else in the world. But even a Y man can't produce an instrument that doesn't exist, and so this one had to go back to Private Tender and suggest a substitute—one more in the world of substitutes that France was in those days.

"Here's a cigar box." he offered, "and some spool wire. Come on; I'll help you make it." And make it they did, and Private Tender was able to extract such compelling music from the instrument that he was drafted, with his panatella fiddle, into a soldier show that went touring France.

1935

The one string cigar box fiddle is often called a "Japanese fiddle" or "Jap fiddle" from experiences such as this reported in the *Oakland Tribune* May 3, 1935. The instrument heard on the short wave may not have been made from a cigar box, and it may have had more than one string. It was the interpretation of English soldiers and their ingenuity that led to the creation of the "Jap fiddle."

Unknown one-string "Jap" fiddle player

Short Wavers Get Japanese Rhythm

At the present time two stations seem to be doing most of the broadcasting from Japan, and these two are JVN, 10.60 megs and JVM, 10.74 megs. JVN does not seem to be operating on any fixed regular schedule and may be heard at various times from 3 to 9 p.m., relaying JOAK. JVM comes on the air every night at 10:50 and stays on until 11:20 p. m., with a little music and speech, and then leaves the air to return again about 12:30 a.m., with further programs of a startling nature. On Saturday evening when a baseball game is in progress both of these stations broadcast at the same time from about 8, until the last man is out. Although all of the programs are in Japanese they are none the less enjoyable for that reason as the dramatic and musical offerings are entirely different from anything else heard on the air. The orchestras feature what sounds like one siring banjoes, cigar box fiddles and assorted harps, and they play with a wistful fervor that lends enchantment to the strange rythms [sic].

The Outlook, Outlook Pub. Co., 1935

...they cannot make the music themselves unless they can draw upon the abundance of musical talent in their respective unites (many of which have no bands at all) and unless the have the instruments. Here and there in the Army or Navy a man ingeniously has manufactured an instrument to supply the need. A corporal of "the Buffaloes," for example, made a "one-dolin" out of a cigar-box, a stick of wood, and one wire string.

156

1940

A real picture postcard from the 1940s shows German prisoners, one of whom is playing a one-string cigar box Jap fiddle. A sign behind the ensemble reads, "Attention! Soldiers!"

Attention! Soldiers! Ensemble!

1968

From the September 22, 1968 edition of the *Albuquerque Journal*, we learn of Hector Garcia, born in Havana in 1930:

> classical guitarist and artist in residence at the University of New Mexico, is launching an additional phase of his colorful career, following a summer in Spain, studying with Emllio Pujol, That famous "maestro," now in advancing years, received 25 guitarists from all over the world in

the three month course sponsored by the Spanish government. A concert artist, widely acclaimed in both Europe and America, Garcia did his first composing during the long months he was held in Castro's dungeon prison, along with 1113 other men captured in the ill-fated Bay of Pigs invasion of 1961. Using bits of wire and scraps of tin, with an old cigar box, Garcia fashioned a "kind of a guitar" to bolster the spirits of his fellow prisoners... and during this time he also composed several concertos and other concert pieces. These were confiscated by the Castro government, following the release of the prisoners ransomed by the U. S. government. Using some of the crude instruments, self fashioned in prison, the group appeared on the Ed Sullivan television show shortly after their liberation.

Children's Music Education

*"In the beginner's mind
there are many possibilities,
in the expert's mind there
are few."*
    - Shunryu Suzuki

1917

A change in perception of the cigar box violin begins to take place at this time. As vaudeville wanes in popularity and motion pictures take its place, the cigar box violin finds a new home in childhood education. As reported in the March 28, 1917 *Lancaster Daily Eagle*, two simultaneous meetings of the Ohio O. A. B. C. convention features:

Special music furnished by Miss Margaret L. Matheny, whistler, nine years old, and her sister Thelma at the piano, was a feature of both meetings. The wonderful little warbler, who has been here before, whistled several selections which delighted her audience. They are daughters of Stacia Matheny. Mr. Davis also played some hymns on his one stringed fiddle made from a

cigar box and a three cent string, first at one
church and then at the other.

And on May 11, 1917, *The Daily Courier* of Connellsville
PA writes that:

> Prof. Davis of Philadelphia is making his first trip
> to this county. He has with him his wonderful
> "one string fiddle," which he himself made at a
> total cost of three cents cut of a cigar box and a
> banjo string! He will have charge of the music for
> both sessions.

1921

Clearly written for children, on June 24, 1921, *The
Sandusky Star Journal* claims, cigar box fiddles are easy to
make. The illustration printed and the instructions, such
as they are, are painfully insulting. [See Historic Cigar
Box Instrument Plans]

Another sign of the times is reported in *The Logansport
Morning Press*, July 21, 1921; simple instruments in the
hands of children were now commonplace for musical
education.

CHURCH MEMBERS HOLD PICNIC

> The members of the M. E. choir; enjoyed a social
> evening at the church Tuesday evening. Music was
> furnished by the Galveston orchestra composed
> of cigar box fiddles, sliding trombones, gourd
> cornets, tin flutes and fifes, paste board cellos,
> Jews harps and other musical instruments too
> numerous to mention.

The stunts performed by each one afforded a great deal of fun. It certainly was amusing to hear Bessie Wiuinger bray like a mule, Lee Logan to sing "K-K-Katy," Elsie and Ada Rodibaugh play a piano solo, Vesper Jones cackle like a hen, Mildred Wood bark like a dog, Vergil Barnhart meow like a cat, Margaret Kitchell and Elizabeth Beeson play a piano duet, Beulah Clearwater give a reading and to see Elsie Streeter lead the orchestra, and Rev. Sanks to try to repeat the Twenty Third Psalm; Ice cream and cake were served. The evening was ended in a big sing with Rev. Sanks at the piano.

1922

In 1922, Satis Coleman published her definitive work, *Create Music For Children*, which focused on teaching music to children through the construction of their own primitive instruments made from a variety of materials, including cigar boxes. Coleman's work, radical during its time, sought to teach music first through the experience of producing music rather than a through a barrage of exercises and learning to read musical notation off a piece of paper. [See Satis Coleman]

1923

While the family in this photograph is not known, this photograph from 1923 shows a group playing a variety of homemade instruments. Two are seen clearly playing one-string fiddles made from what look to be a broom handle and cigar box.

Two One-String Cigar Box Violins Ensemble

1932

From *The Galveston Daily News*, May 8, 1932:

Lincoln, Neb., May 7.—OT—Talk about Tin Pan Alley. Here's a man who doesn't need even a tin pan to make music. Just the alley will do.

Dr. Charles C. Weidemann, given almost anything that will vibrate audibly, will produce a musical instrument. Step into his office in the teachers' college at the University of Nebraska and you will see slabs of rock, bits of hose, funny sticks, an old mop and fruit jars. Almost before you know it, if you mention music, the professor will be playing a solo on a 25c marimba. But his favorite, is the "musical box." It's about an inch and a quarter by an inch and a half in size, made of white pine about the thickness of cigar box wood, and open at one end.

The Inventor opens and closes his hand over the open end while thumping, the box with the other hand. And it hums any tune with the utmost sincerity. Another of his creations is the "mop-o-phone." "It's my mother's mop stick with one wire string attached to it. A violin-bow and a cigar box are used to play it"

He advocates construction of the instrument as a diversion.

"Recently." he relates, "a group of 17 lads learned to play a hymn in six-part music upon bottles during two practice periods of about 30 minutes each."

1935

In the February/March issue of *Popular Homecraft*, plans for "How to Make a Cigar Box Violin" are published. Given the multiple sources that appear around this time featuring easy-to-build instruments for children, this is not surprising. However, it should be noted that these are plans for a full 4-string instrument. Similar plans or evidence of cigar box violins had fewer strings because they were easier to play. The bow often would not have clear access to the outer strings from the square box. For that reason, cigar box violins were often limited to three strings or less. [See Historic Cigar Box Instrument Plans]

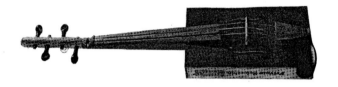

1936

Published in 1936, *Whittling and Woodcarving*, by E. J. Tangerman, Dover Publications, Inc., New York, p 36, 40. Tangerman remembers making cigar box fiddles in his youth:

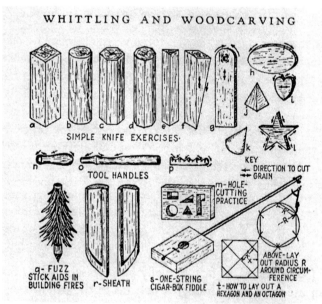

Tangerman's Whittling and Woodcarving Illustration

As a youngster I had a lot of fun with the one-string or Chinese fiddle made of a cigar box and a broomstick. Whittle out a hole just large enough to fit the broomstick at each end of the box and a larger hole in the bottom. Put the broomstick through until about an inch sticks out of the base, then wedge it in place and nail the box top shut. Drill a hole through the upper end of the broomstick for a key and a slot at right angles to it for the string. Then make a little triangle (see *e*) for the bridge just back of the large hole in the cigar box, whittle out a key (*h* on top of a tapered *b*), run your string from the base up around the key, adjust the bridge and tune up. The cats will leave.

Jenkins Orphanage

According to *The South Carolina Encyclopedia*:

Jenkins Orphanage was established in 1891 by Rev. Daniel J. Jenkins in Charleston, South Carolina. Jenkins was a former slave turned minister who, upon stumbling across homeless youths, decided to organize an orphanage for young African American children.

The orphanage took in donations of musical instruments, and later hired two local Charleston musicians, P.M. "Hatsie" Logan and Francis Eugene Mikell, to tutor the boys in music. Upon its establishment, it became the only black instrumental group organized in South Carolina. The band's debut was on the streets of Charleston with the permission of the mayor, police chief, and Chamber of Commerce. The Jenkins Orphanage Band, wearing discarded Citadel uniforms, performed throughout the United States and even toured England raising money for the support of the orphanage. It played in inaugural parades of Presidents Theodore Roosevelt and William Taft.

Photo from the estate of Francis Eugene Mikell shows a one-string cigar box guitar and one-string broom (lower left)

It is possible that, given the few recordings of street performances that exist, an early recording of a cigar box guitar from Jenkins Orphanage Band could exist. Such a recording would predate the recording of Beans Hambone's "Beans" around 1929. Sadly, I have not been able to locate any such recording of a Jenkins Orphanage Band that features a cigar box guitar.

In *The Olean Evening Times*, March 8, 1929 Arthur Dean writes:

> Real music has to start from the soul. The boy who tortures a tune on a cigar box banjo of his

own manufacture is far closer to the real spirit of music than the poor lad whose fond mama stands him up before her patient friends and makes him scrape through a masterpiece on his violin.

The music of the banjo boy may be crude but it is generated deep down inside of him. It's the boy's soul which is speaking.

Dean continues in *The Olean Evening Times* on March 11, 1929, writing about the use of creativity in the home to keep children happy. Dean follows in the footsteps of Satis Coleman in getting children to create their own musical instruments and learn to play on their creations:

The happiest families are those where everyone is busy at creative work... Now music, through the radio, is entering your soul as it is mine. And it's because I want our boys and girls to get, early in life that opportunity for musical expression which is in the soul of all of us that I am writing this series of articles about music for children.

A group of ingenious youngsters will build up quite an orchestra out of these odd instruments. Assume that Jack is the oldest and most expert at making things so he has a cheese-box banjo. Brother Frank has a marimba fashioned out of stray slabs of wood. And sister Nancy plays the musical glasses—merely ordinary tumblers tuned with water. Jack's chum, Ned, has some elderberry panpipes. Nancy's friend plays the cigar box zither. And of coarse they need a drum, to Ned's little brother pounds out the rhythm on one he has made from a candy pail. Then, just to give the orchestra foundation, maybe mother or big sister comes in and plays the piano. Can't you imagine the grand tunes they are able to make? Don't smile folks. The heart of music is right here.

They learn the very simplest tunes, at the start, maybe a melody of three notes only. After that, one of four, then five and so on till soon they are pounding out familiar tunes like veterans and even improvising their own. But they will always be playing tunes, not scales and exercises, but tunes and always together. That's the thing to hold their interest. And fun, oh boy.

The book of Mrs. Coleman's which I mentioned last week is the guide in making these homemade instruments. And what tunes children can play on them! Frankly the book is quite irresistible, even to a supposedly sedate grown-up like myself. I got safely through the chapters on rattles and drums. When I came to musical glasses I simply couldn't resist and presently I was rummaging around the pantry to find glasses of the right tones so I might play "Hot Cross Buns."

Now I have designs on an empty cigar box. Now little Cigar Box, don't you cry—you'll be a banjo by-and-by.

1935

An article by J.C. Van Abburgh appears in *The Daily Inter Lake, Kalispell, Montana* on October 22, 1935. Van Abburgh's views are related to those of Coleman, but unlike D.C. Beard, who wanted urban children to unleash their inner savage, Abburgh posits that through musical education, even on homemade instruments, "good ethical character" is built.

PUBLIC SCHOOL ORCHESTRA

In accordance with the nature of children we find them striving ever to express themselves on some kind of musical instrument. They sing, whistle and in time, try to play some mechanical musical instrument. It is often an instrument of their own making.

Common instruments that children make and ask others to make for them are: one-tone whistles, whistles with slide, sea shell horns, comb and paper harps, cigar box fiddles, and tin can drums.

The play whistles are the beginning of the woodwind instruments men have tried to perfect.

A stick or two sticks are often used to beat rhythm on almost any kind of object that will give back a sound. The knife and fork are, sometimes struck against the table or plate. Here we have the beginning of the percussion section.

Children, in their play, often discover that by properly vibrating their lips by passing the breath through a small opening of their lips and into a gas pipe or a sea shell they can produce a sound, of a certain pitch. This is the beginning of the brass section.

In stretching a string, wire, or rubber to a certain length and tension they learn the possibilities of their play instrument. This is the beginning of the string section.

Since it is natural for children to try to express themselves through the medium of sound on some mechanical instrument it is the duty of the older generation to provide instruments and instruction in their use.

The Orchestra movement tries to select students with some musical interests and aptitudes, place them with the instrument most fitted to their interests and capacities and to give special instruction in the use of the instruments. Private study must go hand and hand with the orchestra work.

We help the child to realize the different units of society by actually taking part in an organization that starts with the individual and includes the local school, the country, state and nation. While the student is away from home proper guidance he puts, his best foremost. His ideals and habits of conduct are directly affected by participation in social life. They must cooperate with each other in solving the problems, of food and transportation when the orchestra makes a trip. When the orchestras of the various towns come together for a district orchestra meeting, the students have a chance to learn the value of the kind of social work done by the various institutions as the school, church, lodge, chamber of commerce, Kiwanis, Rotary, etc. Further, every students [sic] feels a social responsibility in representing his school.

An instrument is a very exacting thing to deal with and its use in the orchestra aids the student in acquiring the social trails of honesty, thrift, industry, congeniality, courtesy, loyalty, sportsmanship, and responsibility. These socially acquired traits go to make up ones traits of ethical character.

Music is a great comfort to the home. There is enjoyment in participation in the production of music. To listen to, or watch someone perform whom you are vitally interested in, will gave enjoyment and add to the happiness of the home. Give the child a chance to play music in the home and his home life will interest him more. The child must be interested in his home and kept from an undue amount of the street life. When the child grows up and is a member of a home of his own the music will be an interest worth continuing.

The orchestra gives vocational guidance and training to a select few. Hence we find the Public School Orchestra lending its influence to help, the institution realize the aims of health, citizenship, ethical character, worthy home membership, worthy use of leisure and vocation.

Kalispell now has orchestra work in both the grade and high schools. Our new auditorium will accommodate a larger orchestra than heretofore. Every parent that has a musical child should take advantage of the opportunities provided.

J. G. VAN AMBURGH,
Director Flathead
Symphony Orchestra

1936

In this photograph from the Cigar Box Guitar Museum in the front row, second from the left, a woman can be seen holding a one-string cigar box instrument. Handwritten at the bottom of the photograph are the words "Music History Class, Sept 1936 with our primitive instruments." This curious collection of handmade, primitive instruments is another indication of the influence of the musical teachings of Satis Coleman.

The handwritten note on the bottom of this photo reads, "Music History Class of Sept., 1936 with our primitive instruments"

1938

From the *Parade Of Youth*, May 1, 1938:

Music 'Fan' Makes 'Cello Of Old Box

The first 'cello Douglas Feaver ever saw was the one he made!

"Music has been my hobby ever since I was 6," writes Douglas, 16, from West Hill Ontario, Canada, "and everything that came into the house in the way of music fascinated me. Once I made a sort of xylophone out of jam jars and water.

"I decided one day that an old stick, a cigar box and the strings from a tennis racket would make some smart noise. Jokingly I told a neighbor, who has a well-equipped workshop, that I was making a 'cello. He took me at my word, offered me the use of the shop, and I had to go through with it.

"Never having seen a 'cello. I drew up the plans myself from my sister's violin, just doubling the measurements, and they turned out surprisingly accurate!"

But the cigar box and tennis strings were out. "My 'cello has a pine sound box, hand-carved birch neck and scroll, mahogany fingerboard — and real 'cello strings," he says.

1976

In the October 17, 1976 issue of the *Oakland Tribune*, "Home's Where Piano Is," and "It's Grand," Chuck Anderson reports on Marilynne Blanc. Blanc appears to be following in the footsteps of Satis Coleman with respect to music education through multicultural influences, and by getting children involved through building their own instruments for performance:

A cellist and music educator, makes no pretense of keeping a fancy home. She doesn't have the time – or the inclination. "This is a functional house," she said, sitting amid the clutter of dozens of musical instruments in the pine-paneled living-dining area of a pleasant, simple home in wooded Orinda. This contemporary residence is much more than a living space. It is the activity center for the tremendously varied musical interests of Mrs. Blanc and the work of her husband, Bob, a high school English teacher...

Her work as a music consultant in the Orinda Unified School District is as dear to Mrs. Blanc as her job as cellist with the Oakland Symphony. Under her supervision, Orinda teachers help students learn to make flutes from sections of garden hose, xylophones from obsidian spikes and bells from flower pots. "Each instrument that the children have made from available materials teaches them the evolution of instruments used by professional musicians today," said Mrs. Blanc. She often has materials spread around the living room as she figures out a new instrument for kids to build. On the patio is a tent that houses her workshop – also for the school projects – during good weather.

One enters the Blanc home from an expansive wooden deck. The front door is nothing special. But once you step inside, it is like a casually run museum... hanging on the walls and spread on the furniture, are dozens of odd-looking stringed and wind instruments. Proudly displayed are Romanian pan pipes, a Hungarian zither, an African harp, an antique Italian mandolin and other equally unusual items. Mrs. Blanc reaches and grabs a squarish, light-colored instrument, kind of like an elongated cigar box with a guitar neck attached. She sits in a chair and begins to play it like she would her cello.

Marginalization

"Books serve to show a man that those original thoughts of his aren't very new at all."

-Abraham Lincoln

The cigar box guitar goes through a period in the mid-twentieth century where, as a serious instrument, it is ignored or marginalized as substandard. Here are the rubber band guitars, noise makers, toys and play things of children – not the simple and playable homemade instruments of Coleman's students. At the same time, cigar box instruments survive in the hands of adults as trench art in WWII where they were formed in desperation for entertainment. The idea remained alive as an instrument here, however, knowing that they were sub-standard and would be gladly replaced should a more legitimate version of the same instrument become available.

1926

From the *Syracuse Herald*, October 10, 1926, in perhaps what is a sign of things to come, the cigar box violin is the subject of humor:

Willie Weakbean Writes a Letter to the Editor
BY PROF. GEORGE SMITH
"How I Built My Own Violin At Home"
An essay by Willie Weakbean as written for the
Child Musicians Corner in the "Popular
Mechanics Magazine"

Dear Editor:
When I read your wonderful encouragement on how to make homemade things at home, I decided to build my violin. I had always longed to take violin lessons, and my father said if I could build me a good violin and earn the money for my lessons, he would be glad to help me study. I believe that the story of my success and the details of my efforts would be encouraging to other young people and I am glad to try and inspire others just as your wonderful encouragement inspired me.

When I began to build my violin I found that the first thing I needed was a good cigar box for the sounding box. I suppose that a good shoe box would have been almost as good, but I did want my first violin to be a good one. I want to say right here that a good cigar box is absolutely necessary in building a violin. If old Stradivarius had only had a good cigar box, he could have improved on his model enough to have interested the Italian Chamber of Commerce in putting out some publicity for him.

Well, as everyone knows, a bridge is one of the most important things on a violin. I was puzzled about a bridge for a long time. I knew Brooklyn Bridge was too big. And the bridge down our road was an old one—pretty much out of shape. I thought of London Bridge then, and remembered that it was falling down and perhaps they would sell me it cheap. So I wrote and asked the Prince of Wales would be [willing to] sell me London Bridge two dollars down and two a month. I got a nice letter back from the Prince himself.

He wrote:
"I am greatly interested, old bean, in your ambitious plan in regard to building your own violin. I think it perfectly ripping. In fact, I think it right topping. Cherio!

"But I can't sell you London Bridge. In the first place, the old bridge is the only one we have in London, and if I sold it the people on the other side of London would never know what the people on the other side of London were doing. Besides, I find that falling off London Bridge is more fun than falling off horses, so there!

"Bully for you, Willie. Best luck.
"THE PRINCE"

So, as you see, I got a nice answer from him. But I still had to find a bridge, and it took me some months to find one, though I finally did, in a town near ours.

The next thing I had to, find was cat-gut for my strings. We had a good old tom at home, but he was quite a pet, and I hated to string him. So I had to chase around after some good cats. You would be surprised to know how hard it is to find a cat with a good G string in her. Now, of course, I keep several cats on hand all the time. A first class E string cat is worth money.

It wasn't long after that that I finished with the violin itself. Then I had to get after a bow.

The wooden handle for a bow is easy to make. I just sawed off an old broom for my first one. Later I became more fussy and used part of an old golf club. But the hard part of a bow is the horse hair. We didn't have a bit of horsehair in the house.

Finally it struck me that it would be clever to just buy a horse and then have it in case my bow kept wearing out. So I got one and from then on I had plenty of horse hair from his tail to use on my bow.

I want to say though that any young people desiring any horsehair for their violin bow had better not ever try to pull a hair from any horses tail while they are standing behind a horse. Because, if they do, they will soon be playing a harp and you don't need a bow for that.

My teacher and all my friends think that my violin is the best one in this town. My teacher told me that if I would paste a little slip saying "Made in Cremona 1767 by Stradivarius" on the inside of the cigar box that he bet I could get ten dollars for it any day from Kreisler if Kreislor was drunk. He said there wore lots of Stradivarius violins loose in this country not half as fine as mine.

I am progressing in my playing nicely. Now I can play all of "The Maiden's Prayer" by heart, and have learned to imitate weasels, cows, and congressmen on my Stradivarius. I am so happy and I think that if lots of little boys and girs [sic] who read your magazine would just have the encouragement to buy a horse and a cat and a cigar box, they woud [sic] soon be just as happy as I am.

Very sincerely yours,
WILLIE WEAKBEAN

ONE MAN'S TRASH

1926

Even with the cigar box guitar becoming an object of ridicule for the entertainment of children, the cigar box guitar continues to thrive in minds of adults as evidenced in the publication and review of *Going to the Stars* by (Nicholas) Vachel Lindsay in this year. According to the *Outline of American Literature*:

> Vachel Lindsay was a celebrant of small-town midwestern populism and creator of strong, rhythmic poetry designed to be declaimed aloud. His work forms a curious link between the popular, or folk, forms of poetry, such as Christian gospel songs and vaudeville (popular theater) on the one hand, and advanced modernist poetics on the other. An extremely popular public reader in his day, Lindsay's readings prefigures "Beat" poetry readings of the post-World War II era that were accompanied by jazz.

> To popularize poetry, Lindsay developed what he called a "higher vaudeville," using music and strong rhythm. Racist by today's standards, his famous poem "The Congo" (1914) celebrates the history of Africans by mingling jazz, poetry, music, and chanting. At the same time, he immortalized such figures on the American landscape as Abraham Lincoln ("Abraham Lincoln Walks at Midnight") and John Chapman ("Johnny Appleseed"), often blending facts with myth.

Lindsay was known for playing sometimes bizarre musical accompaniment during his poetry readings. I have not, however, found an account of a performance with a cigar box instrument. Plausibility aside, I have no

182

proof of such a performance, so this is pure conjecture on my part. Initially I was encouraged to have this idea when I found a partial review of Lindsay's book in the *Book Review Digest* (1926, page 420), it is suggested by the reviewer that:

> I confess to a great weakness for Vachel Lindsay. Here is a minstrel, a real singer. How cleverly, with what joyous craftsmanship he wrings music out of a few wires and a cigar box!

This brief snippet set me off to explore a new mystery. I needed to read the rest of the review, as well as explore Lindsay's work. I was initially disappointed because, as it turns out, Lindsay's *Going To The Stars*, for which the review was written, never mentions cigar box music. At best, the book review uses the culturally acceptable idea for this era that the cigar box guitar is something less than perfect, but intriguing for its ability to manage to hold itself together and craft a few well chosen notes from such simple construction. After reading the rambling prose in Lindsay's *Going To The Stars* and seeing the illustrations and hieroglyphs (as Lindsay described them), the comparison made in the review is clear when the review is read in its entirety. For this, I consulted the *Independent,* from which the snippet in the *Book Review Digest* was taken:

> Both Sandburg and Lindsay are by way of being musicians. The prosiest looking of their poems is built for singing. The new tempos and musical idioms of America have contributed something new to the lyric Muse… I confess to a great weakness for Vachel Lindsay. Here is a minstrel, a real singer. How cleverly, with what joyous craftsmanship he wrings music out of a few wires

and a cigar box! How accurately he adjusts word
to time and rhythm to air! ...Two singers of the
sunburnt West, each contributes in his way
something real and something valuable to the new
American tradition. Let us, therefore, give thanks
for them.

In a burst of clever writing, the reviewer came up with
one of the few known metaphors using the cigar box
guitar. Sandburg's and Lindsay's work were not about
cigar box instruments directly, but their musical prose
suggested to the reviewer the same effective simplicity
that a cigar box instrument represents. Further
investigation into Sandburg revealed a pleasant surprise.
In the review, Sandburg is only mentioned as being a
musician, in a later collection of Sandburg's works,
Poetry for Young People, the introduction mentions:

Poet Carl Sandburg, born January 6, 1878, in
Galesburg Illinois, Sandburg was a wonderer who
always wanted to try new things and go to new
places... He loved music and experimented with
homemade musical instruments such as a willow
whistle and a cigar-box banjo.

1938

The April 1938 issue of *Scientific American* has an
advertisement, Bass Bargaingram, where president
Charles Bass mentions:

Of course you can take swell pictures with a $5
camera... you can also get good violin music out
of a cigar box contraption... but better from a
'Strad'. We sell the $5 models... but know that

you get more lasting satisfaction from the better kind – and it is much easier to recommend them.

After reading Vachel Lindsay's *Going to the Stars*, and the book review from 1926, this passage is only the second instance I could find in my research where a cigar box instrument is used as analogy for crafting something suitable from something common – a cigar box. It establishes the fact that the audience understands the cigar box guitar or violin as something suitable, but not the finest quality.

1942

Searching through the contents of both the Cigar Box Guitar Museum, and Tony Hyman's National Cigar Museum (on the Made from boxes page) it appears that a single work by Raymond James Stuart depicts two variations on a single subject. According to Hyman:

> Lavish living commercial magazine and calendar artist Raymond James Stuart, who worked from 1921 to 1962, frequently portrayed boys (usually with dogs) playing cigar box instruments. Stuart was known for his cute kid paintings, tho [sic] he once confided to a reporter that he couldn't stand "the noisy, squirmy little buggers."

Pictured first, an earlier version of the same subject, copyright 1942, and attributed to J. F. Stuart, is an illustration of violinist Fritz Kreisler, an Austrian-born violinist and composer who was one of the most famous violinists of his day, hanging on the boy's wall. Sheet music to Yankee Doodle rests on the floor between to boy's feet.

185

Pictured second, the 1946 Stuart calendar features the same cigar box violinist; however, in this illustration, we see a personalized Christmas card of famous Russian concert violinist David Rubinoff whose autographed picture hangs on the boy's wall.

From the Original Painting   ASPIRING GENIUS   Artist J. F. Stuart

Two Stuart artworks, with different violinists hanging on the wall

1945

A brief review and suggested reading appears for Burmans's *Blow for a Landing* again in the September 1,

1945 issue of *The Stars and Stripes Magazine*, in the GI Bookshelf section, apparently given in a T-series [T probably being short for "Title" then followed by an index number] "to cover a myriad of subjects to whet the reading appetites of a wide range of literary enthusiasts—from those who find pleasure in humor and adventure, to the GIs with a yen for farming and those who enjoy the mysteries of a king's court and harem."

"Blow for a Landing" (T-27) by Ben Lucien Burman, is Americana at its best. Burman writes of the Mississippi, and Willow Joe with his cigar box guitar. It's a "lazy river" book, replete with dialect and folk tales.

From the *La Crosse Tribune And Leader-Press*, May 25, 1945:

Thrifty Youth Is Manufacturer Of His Own Guitar

New Amsterdam, Wis. – (Special) – "To make the good better and the better best is the height of my ambition."

Thus spoke Arlin' Meyer as he cradled his artistically decorated guitar and picked the strings in accompaniment to a favorite tune.

His longing for a guitar developed several years ago but Arlin wasn't spending his good money for an instrument until sure he could master the art of playing it. Hence a cigar box was rigged up on which to test his skill. The purchase of a cheap moled [sic] guitar was his next venture. Without professional training but with diligent practice over a long period of time the young man accomplished what he set out to do. Thus governed in a decision that he was now ready for something better he went about making a guitar in his spare time. Built according to his own specifications and with only a few tools with which to work he completed a fine-looking guitar, narrow strips of leather cut from a discarded purse cleverly conceal the seams on the top and bottom of the instrument where the wood was joined and glued together. This formed a setting for the design of colored sets salvaged from pins, brooches and buttons.

Admittedly still an amateur, Arlin nevertheless has plans underway for a still better and bigger guitar.

1948

Plans for a Cigar Box Violin by W.J. Sutherland are published in the February/March issue of *Science and Mechanics*. [See Historic Cigar Box Instrument Plans]

It should come as no surprise that also during this time that many of the blues greats started out with cigar box guitars during this era. Jug bands already made homemade instruments *en vogue*. To make a cigar box guitar, or what have you, was really in fashion at this time. Like the trench art instruments of WWII, these cigar box instruments of blues musicians where only temporary. For, once a proper instrument was obtained the cigar box variant was never used again.

1949

As reported in *The Progress*, October 20, 1949, evangelist Rev. Ralph A. Creider played a variety of instruments ranging from a xylophone made from 40 empty whiskey bottles, a set of singing bells ranging from a dinner bell to a ships gong, and tuned wine glasses:

Unusual Music Instruments Are Played by Evangelist

The one-stringed cigar-box broomstick fiddle that was played over the Gospel Echoes program, heard station WCPA Sunday morning from 8:30 to 9 a.m. was also played in Tuesday's service. This instrument is made from a cigar box which has been carved upon to give it the tone principles of a violin. The box is attached to a broomstick and has only one string.

1951

Relegated to children's play things, the cigar box guitar degenerates to a set of rubber bands around an old box as published in *The Post-Standard*, October 6, 1951. [See Historic Cigar Box Instrument Plans]

On September 27, 1951, Charles Schulz featured an eager Charlie Brown on cigar box banjo accompanying Schroeder. Schroeder did not appreciate Chuck's primitive sound.

Further evidence that the cigar box guitar is becoming marginalized as a toy is seen in the cover art of *Ha Ha Comics*, Issue 80, published in October, 1951. Based in the characters therein, this appears to be Robespierre is serenading a fair maiden of a cat. Neither the female cat nor the cigar box guitar appears inside the comic.

Ha Ha Comics makes cigar box guitars no laughing matter

191

1952

In an illustration published May 11, 1952, Charles Schulz shows that Charlie Brown is ready for concert performance on his cigar box violin. Surprisingly, Chuck takes the opportunity for a solo performance.

1953

On October 1, 1953 Charles Schulz publishes another Charlie Brown strip featuring the cigar box banjo.

In a strip published April 23 of this same year, Schulz has Schroeder challenge the idea of playing Beethoven on a toy violin. Apparently crushed by this statement, Charlie Brown is never again seen playing cigar box violins, banjos, or toy instruments of any kind in another Peanuts cartoon.

1954

From the *Oakland Tribune*, May 9, 1954, the rubber band cigar box guitar continues to appear. [See Historic Cigar Box Instrument Plans]

1964

Published in the *Fitchburg (Mass.) Sentinel*, January 24, 1964, Hal Boyle writes about "A discard list of things most of us could do without" including:

> All college graduates who create folk music by beating on a washboard, blowing into a jug, or playing on a cigar box fiddle.

1967

In 1967, Betty Horvath published *Jasper Makes Music*. Horvath's book is a children's story about a young boy, Jasper, who wants a real guitar of his own. Without money to buy exactly the guitar he wants, he tries to make his own from a cigar box. It didn't sound like a real guitar. To him, "It sounded like an old cigar box strung with rubber bands, and Jasper put it down."

Fermin Rocker's illustration from Jasper Makes Music

1971

Richard Scarry's *Best Stories Ever* features the illustrated story of Chicken Little. Ducky Lucky tragically was eaten by Foxy Loxy and lost a cigar box guitar as a result. Copyright for Scarry's stories go back as far as 1950.

Foxy Loxy walked with Ducky Lucky.
Foxy Loxy ate Ducky Lucky.

In 1971, The "Country Bear Jamboree" opened to an enthusiastic response as one of the original attractions at the Magic Kingdom at Walt Disney World, Florida. On the reverse of Cousin Zeb and Zeke's postcard reads:

> Little ol' Tennessee Bear, signed by legendary Disneyland artist Marc Davis, mint unused postcard from the Summer of 1970 Disneyland promoting the about to open Walt Disney World October 1971 opening of Country Bear Band Jamboree. First sold in New Orleans Square, this was a part of a 16 card set later sold in 8 piece sets in the Teddy Beara's Swing'n Arcade located where the Winnie the Pooh Candy shops are now.

Legendary Disney artist Marc Davis designed the show, as well as The Haunted Mansion, Pirates of the Caribbean, Carousel of Progress, and It's A Small World, The Jungle Cruise, America Sings (to name a few). Show is now long gone, and this card is long out of print.

LITTLE OL' TENNESSEE BEAR
PLAYS ON A HOME-MADE "THING";
MADE IT SPECIAL FOR THE BEAR BAND
JUST TO HELP THOSE CRITTERS SWING.

THE COUNTRY BEAR BEAU BRUMMELL
IS A BEAR THEY CALL THE DUDE;
HIS BOW-TIE'S POLKA DOTTED
BUT IT'S MOSTLY STAINED WITH FOOD.

Marc Davis adds his signature to Little Ol' Tennessee Bear

This is a reproduction of one of the original sketches used to create The "Country Bear Jamboree" in the Magic Kingdom's Frontierland. From these drawings, Disney Imaginineers sculpted miniature scale models and then full-size figures. Through the magic of Audio-Animatronics, the performers were "brought-to-life" to sing, strum guitars and perform in a wild and zany frontier musical.

1975

In *Prof. Hammerfingers' Indestructible Toys*, published in October 1975, Steve Ross presents plans for another rubber band banjo with a non-functional wooden piece for a "neck." [See Historic Cigar Box Instrument Plans]

Country Bear Jamboree — A real foot-stompin' hoe down featuring the Five Bear Rugs, greets visitors to Frontierland

In this time period of cigar box instruments being the object of comical shtick, there is a ray of hope. The cigar box as a makeshift instrument is still valid, for in this same year, *Foxfire Volume 3* contains a chapter on banjos and dulcimers. In a section on the history of the banjo, the book mentions:

> An article by C.J. Hyne in the December 15, 1888 issue of the "Boys Own Paper" [reprinted in the March 1974 issue of Mugwumps] says, "With rapid strides it improved in form. First a wooden hoop, and then a metal one; first a rough skin for the drum, then the best parchment; first nails to

hold it on, then neatly made tension screws. At one time the strings were made of anything that came to hand; now they are formed from the 'intestines of the agile cat.'"

Though all banjos prior to 1880 were fretless, demand for fretted ones by minstrel banjoists at that time cause several manufacturers to put them on the market.

Echoing the "no rules" approach of the cigar box guitar, the authors of *Foxfire Volume 3* observe:

There is so much variety in banjo construction that it would seem as thought *anything* goes as long as it "rings."

Several of the interviews in *Foxfire Volume 3* feature Appalachian banjo makers who mention early experimentation with cigar boxes and other found objects. Ernest Franklin recalls his early banjos: "Well, I'll tell you, the first one I ever made - you've seen your wooden cigar boxes? Well, I made one out a square wooden cigar box. I didn't have no patterns or nothing to go by. I just thought that up myself." M. C. Worley told of his first banjo that was made from a cigar box. "It rang pretty good too," according to Worley. As he began to make them regularly, he moved away from the old patterns and began to experiment.

A highlight, for me as an instrument maker, comes from the interview with Dave Sturgill in *Foxfire Volume 3* in which Sturgill offers an excellent formulation of the motivation to create music from found objects. Sturgill elaborates on the use of found objects and available tools, and also mentions poverty as a motivator. As a young boy:

> Dave made his first banjo because he wanted one and was too poor to buy it. He took a plywood packing crate, set it in the creek until it came apart, and then wrapped a strip of its thin wood veneer around a five-gallon can and held it in place with rubber bands until it dried to form the hoop. Then he whittled the neck out with a pocketknife.

> As Dave tells the story: "I knew who was president [of the company from which he retired] at that time because I'd made it a point to find out. So I reminded him [an old friend that he had worked with] which one it was. I said, 'Now that wasn't even thirty years ago, and you're not even sure who the president of the company was when you started.' I says, 'Think about this a little bit. Twenty years from now, there won't be anybody working for this company that will know you or I either one ever worked for it. But,' I says, 'a hundred years from now, they'll be people who will know I made musical instruments.'"

> There are things that are a lot more important than how big an automobile you've got, or how big your bank account is. I was into it up there [in Washington D.C.]. An hour and a half fighting traffic every morning to get downtown. An hour and a half fighting that traffic every evening to get back. I'd be a nervous wreck every time I got on the job, and I'd be he same way when I got home. And, boy, I started asking myself every day, 'Why? Why? What in the world am I fighting this for?'

Sturgill's comment about knowing that in "a hundred years from now, they'll be people who will know I made musical instruments" is a comment that I've heard often from other cigar box guitar makers. I, too, have felt this same connection to people that I don't know, even to people who have not yet been born. In my own experience, cigar box guitars that I have made, once given to their new owners, are immediately branded a family heirloom, something to be handed down through the generations. For that reason, and to honor the countless and often nameless instrument makers before me who did what they could with what they had, I try to infuse each of my own created instruments with as much originality, creativity, artistry, and genuine musicality as I can.

In the hands and mind of the right person, a cigar box instrument can be much more than just a toy or a prop. There are those that required such a humble beginning. There is a sense of paying your dues from such a humble beginning. In fact, the cigar box guitar for many blues musicians in the Mississippi Delta, crafting such an instrument and playing music was seen as a rite of passage.

Rite of Passage

*"Children would make their
own guitars, see, cause their
daddies didn't want them to
mess with theirs. So they
were hung up out of reach so
the kids couldn't get to
them."*
- Ike Turner

The idea of a owning and playing a cigar box guitar or other instrument as a rite of passage is suggested by Barry Lee Pearson in *Sounds so Good to Me: The Bluesman's Story*. Pearson "continually encountered similar corresponding topics that appeared to be characteristic of the blues musicians' tale in general: their first instrument, their parents' response to their music, how they learned to play, who inspired them." Pearson states that "homemade instruments, while a very real folk tradition, loom larger than life in the bluesman's story. They show the artist interested in music at an early age in the rural South and resourceful enough to do something about it." More importantly, Pearson argues that "instrument construction may be seen as a sign of musical destiny," and, "as a dues-paying reference."

201

Pearson, upon observing many similar accounts from the bluesmen that he interviewed, remarks, "an instrument is needed to begin life as a musician; likewise, the musician's story often begins with an instrument." Those instruments, even ones as simple as a makeshift guitar, are more than a means to an end. They serve "as a vehicle through which the artist can express his soul," and "becomes an extension of himself," or "a second voice."

Pearson makes a remarkable observation when he writes about blues artists and their guitars. He makes a comment that, at first reading, appears to be so fundamental that it is easy to overlook. Pearson emphasizes that the musician and their instrument are connected; in other words, there cannot be one without the other: "Musicians are connected to instruments all their musical life and can even organize an autobiography chronologically around the different guitars they have owned. But of all the instruments a musician runs through, none is so frequently of so reverently spoken of as the first, which, like a first love, is idealized."

Through the course of my own research and as demonstrated throughout this book, blues musicians do not possess a monopoly on the makeshift guitar. In this chapter, I have included snippets taken from various sources that demonstrate the legitimacy of the homemade instrument as the starting point for many musicians. Included here are newsworthy events, or in cases where specific dates are irrelevant, I give a brief synopsis of the player taken from interviews and other primary sources.

Breaking News

ca. 1905

In the midst of vaudevillian stage performances and the early works of blues artists, William Grant Still is a unique example, according to *William Grant Still: A Bio-Bibliography*, by Michael J. Dabrishus, et al. While there is no indication of date, the account of his toy violins could fall around 1905, assuming that he was around the age of 10 years old at the time of their making.

> Still was not always happy over being forced to live a life of culture and manners, but, without his being aware, the noble influences of the church and the Lotus Club were drawing him in to his natural artistic element. He began to gravitate toward music, and to try to make music on his own. Soon, he was fashioning toy violins out of cigar boxes, sticks and cat gut, and trying to play them.

William Grant Still went on to become a prominent composer, an apparently unique accomplishment among those who built and played cigar box instruments. Still's success as a composer dispels the myth that cigar box instruments were relegated to the poor blues musician or gimmicks used on the stages of vaudeville:

> William Grant Still (May 11, 1895 - December 3, 1978) was an African-American classical composer who wrote more than 150 compositions. He was the first African-American to conduct a major American symphony orchestra, the first to have a symphony of his own (his first symphony)

performed by a leading orchestra, the first to have an opera performed by a major opera company, and the first to have an opera performed on national television. He is often referred to as "the dean" of African-American composers.

ca. 1908

From Paul Oliver's *Savannah Syncopators*, an account of Big Bill Broonzy recalls that his makeshift instruments sounded and played well enough to entertain:

> When I was about ten years old I made a fiddle out of a cigar box, a guitar out of goods boxes for my buddy Louis Carter, and we would play for the white people's picnics...

Unlikely praise for the cigar box instrument is reported in *The Bucks County Gazette*, April 3, 1908, in a section entitled "For Rapid Reading," this mention reinforces the fact that, when well made, cigar box instruments can sound surprisingly good.

> Very likely the oddest musical instrument in Doylestown is owned by Frank Austin, fireman at the Court House, It is a violin of his own manufacture, made from an ordinary cigar box, but it has a surprisingly good tone.

1912 - Willis Boyce

On rare occasions, early examples of cigar box violins are found intact. Even more rarely, the name of the maker and player are known, such as in this example, made by Willis Boyce, which, according to the marks in pencil on the cigar box, was created on August 19, 1912.

The cigar box from which this violin is made is odd for its warning labels on the back that were in use between 1880-1900, but the tax stamp on the box dates from 1901 to 1910. This is probably an indication of an older box used with a new tax stamp during the interval between these two periods.

In a conversation with Walter Boyce about his father Willis Boyce and his one-string violin, Walter recalls that it "didn't sound too bad."

The only thing I know about it is that my father made it and he used to play it. He played the violin and he studied violin and he used to play all kinds of music. He did play for square dances on Saturday nights and he took it down there as a novelty a few times, and played it there. I guess some people saw it and asked him to play it other places.

There was a little write up in the paper saying that he made it. It's been there as long as I remember and I'm 80 years old. He was born in 1896 and he did study violin while in Brooklyn.

I know it had one string, and one peg, and a bridge. He played it and it didn't sound too bad.

Rite of Passage

My search for more information about Willis Boyce and his cigar box violin led me to an article in *Images of America: Ridgefield.* According to these archives, Willis Boyce was indeed from a musical family. Willis Boyce sang weekly with The Ridgefield Men's Quartet on radio station WICC in Bridgeport for several years. Charlotte Boyce, his wife, was a concert pianist, an organist at St. Stephens Church, as well as a piano teacher, and together, they were popular musicians with the dance bands at Odd Fellows Hall. Perhaps this is the very hall in which Boyce played his one-string cigar box violin.

1914

The November 26, 1914 edition of *The Newark Daily Advocate* reported on the violins made by George S. Conway who constructed his first violin from an oyster tin:

> For twenty years has he been engaged in a work, which with him is a labor of love and had its beginning when he manufactured his first violin from an old fashioned, square, tin oyster can. His father died in Knox county when he was but seven years old and left to drift mostly for himself, he worked for a family in Coshocton county.

> One night a dance was given at the home where he was employed and to the amazement of the child, a queer looking wooden box with strings on it furnished the music for the dancers. This was his first acquaintance with the violin and so closely did he cling to the side of the fiddler and so many questions did he ask that the musician was hampered in his efforts to play for the dance and

the little boy was hurriedly sent to bed. But still he dreamed of the "music box" and the next morning found an old oyster can and made himself a fiddle.

Later he secured a cigar box and some strings and the second effort was a great improvement over the first one. So busily did he fiddle on the new instrument that the members of the family became greatly annoyed and his endeavors had to cease.

He did nothing more with it then until coming to Newark he visited Hubert Dowling in 1912 [possibly 1902 – source damaged]. Mr. Dowling manufactured violins and he became greatly interested in the young man and encouraged him to pursue his efforts in scientific violin construction.

1927

This newsworthy event from the *Mason City Globe-Gazette*, December 29, 1927, foreshadows the children's book *One-String Fiddle* published by Erick Berry in 1939. Is this life imitating art, or art imitating life?

Youans Wins Prize for Being Best C. C. Fiddler

CHARLES CITY, "Dec. 29.—The old fiddlers' contest was largely attended both nights at the Hildreth theater. R. H. Youans won the grand prize for the best all round fiddler. F. W. Clayton won a prize for the most unusual fiddler. His fiddle was made out of a cigar box upon which he played "The Rosary," accompanied by Norma Dietrich, a student at Grinnell college. Mrs. K. Monroe won a prize for the best woman fiddler.

From *The Port Arthur News*, October 26, 1935:

Matches, Pieces Of Hickory, Door Panel And Cigar Box
Used By Port Arthur Youth In Making Fiddle That Plays

Strains of "Turkey In the Straw," "Nellie Gray," and other hillbilly tunes issuing forth from the L. F. Wolf home 'in El Vista community Saturday are the result of an inspiration by Wolf's 18-year-old son, Jackson, "to accomplish something unusual."

Jackson, a slender youth with the shy mannerisms reminiscent of a cowboy come to the city, has put together, in his spare time, a "fiddle," as he calls it, made entirely of scrap pieces of cigar and apple boxes, two pieces of door panel, safety matches and a piece of hickory.

This homemade instrument, from which Jackson is able to "saw out" almost any of the old-fashioned Jigtime tunes which he learned himself in the short space of only three months, was put together in two and a half months' time with a pocket knife and sandpaper his only tools.

Because of the short while in which the youth learned to play the instrument, it would be supposed that he comes from a musical family, but L. F. Wolf, his father, says that his son was the only one born with the knack to pick up the art so quickly.

"I enjoy hillbilly music but I never was able to do much with it myself," he said, "The best I can do is beat time—and it's not so good."

The door panels were used for the top and bottom of the fiddle, with the matches, estimated by Jackson to number about 250, glued together to form the sides. Strips cut from cigar boxes were glued around the insides of the fiddle to furnish a base for the matches. The neck is made from a piece of hickory and the bass board from a piece of apple box.

Still Jackson isn't satisfied. Already he has turned his efforts toward constructing another fiddle on which the sides will be made of tooth picks—to "give it a better tone," as the El Vista youth puts it.

Paul Whiteman writes (filling in for Walter Winchell) in *The Brownsville (Texas) Herald*, July 24, 1935:

One of my fondest memories is a meeting with Stale Bread down in New Orleans.

Stale Bread's real name is Locoume, but no one knows it now. Long ago, while wandering the streets as a blind banjo player, he conceived the idea of founding a Jazz orchestra. There were eight members in that first band, known as: Piggy—Family Haircut — Warm Gravy — Booze Bottle — Seven Colors — Whiskey — Monk.

They had a cheese box for a banjo, a cigar box for a violin, a soap box for a guitar and a half-barrel for a bass fiddle.

Soon they were blocking traffic, and a cop ran them in. The judge, trying not to laugh, ordered them to play in their own defense.

This was a big moment. Stale Bread rose, bowed towards the judge, raised a stick of wood and began. The judge listened patiently. When the terrible din had died he said:

"Stale Bread, you may be a band, but you're a spasm band! Discharged."

1936

We hear about "Stale Bread" again in *The Daily Courier, Connellsville, PA* on March 6, 1936:

"Stale Bread" Lacoume - Traces Jazz Back to '90s

New Orleans, La.—"Stale Bread" Lacoume says New Orleans gave "hot" music to the world and that he should know because he started it all.

Now fifty years old, fat, jolly, blind for 35 years, Lacoume has spent much of his life at music after organizing his own "Spasm Band" of newsboys with homemade instruments.

A group of newsies became familiar with barroom ballads here before the Spanish-American war. Turning a half beer keg into a bass fiddle, a cigar box into a violin, a soap box into a guitar, and so on, the little urchins roved about town for two years playing for handouts.

William Farnum showered them at the opera house with nickels. A police court judge once ordered them to play before him and he dubbed the boys a "spasm band" at the "command performance."

"Ragtime? No; we didn't play ragtime," said Lancoume. "Our stuff was entirely different. I don't think we got it from negro music. We just started putting in the hot stuff and all of a sudden."

1938

From the *Jefferson City Post-Tribune*, August 5, 1938:

TENNESSEE 'FIDDLER' ELECTED TO CONGRESS
Albert Gore Wins Five-Cornered Contest

NASHVILLE, Tenn., Aug. 5—(AP)—Albert Gore, a country boy who learned his ABC's in a little one-room school at Possum Hollow, in Smith county, and who later gained a statewide reputation as a "fiddler," is going to congress.

The 30-year-old Gore, victor in a five cornered race yesterday for the seat made vacant by Rep. J. Ridley Mitchell's unsuccessful candidacy for the U. S. senate, credits in part his "fiddle" for his victory.

Numerous times during the campaign just ended he substituted "fiddling" for speech making in his district.

"I learned to play a fiddle made out of a cigar box when I was just a kid," he said. "About, the first piece I ever learned was 'Shake That Little Foot, Sally,' and I still like that piece best."

Also in this year, according to *All Music Guide to Country*, the Singer / Songwriter Freddie Hart, born December 21, 1933, "before becoming a popular country hitmaker in the early '70s ... at five years old, his grandfather fashioned him a makeshift guitar our of a cigar box and wire from a Model T."

1939

In a bit of art imitating life, Erick Berry publishes *One-String Fiddle* – a story about Irby Jordean and his dog, Billiam, who together with the help of "Old Fiddler" manage to create a one-string cigar box fiddle, write an original tune, and win a fiddlin' contest and ultimately a "sure 'nuff fiddle" as first prize. The story of Irby is very similar to that of the 1927 news of "Youans Wins Prize for Being Best C. C. Fiddler."

Erick Berry's book, while easy to find, even in a first edition copy, is much more difficult to find with an intact set of fold-out plans that were originally pasted in the rear of the book. The plans were pasted in such a way that they would be easy to remove without damage to the book or to the plans. Perhaps that is the reason why the original plans are so difficult to find still attached in the books today. A copy of the plans for "It's Fun To Make A One String Fiddle Like Irby's" is included in the historic plans chapter.

While the recording date is not immediately obvious from the cover art, Erick Berry's one string fiddle would eventually be released on a set of 78 records in unabridged form and read by Paul Wing.

Cigar Box Players

Maya Angelou

In *I Know Why the Caged Bird Sings*, Maya Angelou recalls her youth, after relocating at age three to live with her Grandmother in Stamps, Arkansas. In the early 1900s Angelou's 'Momma' had set up the "Store" based on her successes as a mobile lunch counter operator for sawmen in the lumberyard. The Store was set in the heart of "the Negro area" and soon became the focal point for social events in the town.

> On Saturdays, barbers sat their customers in the shade on the porch of the Store, and troubadours on their ceaseless crawlings through the South leaned across its benches and sang their sad songs of The Brazos while they played juice harps and cigar-box guitars.

Angelou recalls a summer picnic when she was ten years old, "the biggest outdoor event of the year. Everyone was there," including musicians who "brought cigar-box guitars, harmonicas, juice harps, combs wrapped in tissue paper and even bathtub basses."

Angelou, born April 4, 1928, places her memories of these cigar box guitars and their players between 1931 and 1938.

Although this work is intended as a memoir, Angelou nevertheless deploys her considerable literary talents, and in one case, she provides a third example of the cigar box guitar as a metaphor. However, this example is far from flattering, because it invokes unpleasant memories. To Angelou, the sound was repulsive:

> Some families of powhitetrash lived on Momma's farm land behind the school. Sometimes a gaggle of them came to the Store, filling the whole room, chasing out the air and even changing the well-known scents. The children crawled over the shelves and into the potato and onion bins, twanging all the time in their sharp voices like cigar-box guitars.

Big Bill Broonzy

The connection between cigar box and packing crates is also found in the history of the cigar box guitar as briefly mentioned in Paul Oliver's *Savannah Syncopators* from Big Bill Broonzy's (1898-1958) description. Broonzy's account is unusual for the amount of detail he gives about his early instruments. True to form, though, once proper instruments were in hand, the cigar box versions would be left behind.

> When I was about ten years old I made a fiddle out of a cigar box, a guitar out of goods boxes for my buddy Louis Carter, and we would play for the white people's picnics...

A more complete account of "Big Bill of the Blues" from which Oliver's is taken comes from Alan Lomax's definitive work *The Land Where The Blues Began.*

Big Bill Broonzy and twin brother Big Frank Broonzy were born in June of 1893 to sharecroppers Frank Broonzy and Nettie, in Mound Bayou, Mississippi. Despite Big Bill Broonzy's parents wishes for him to become a preacher, he "dropped the plow handles and the Bible, picked up the fiddle and took the devil for his patron."

> One time at a country picnic I heard a musician the folks called See-See Rider playing a cigar-box fiddle. That was the only name I ever knew him to have – See-See Rider. All I know, he was old when I knew him and the best musician in that part of the country. He's been dead now thirty-five years [written in 1940].
>
> See-See Rider used to play at the barrelhouses down home. He lives at Reydell, Arkansas, right on the Arkansas River, and he used to play fiddle all through that country for both white and colored. He had him a homemade band – fiddle, guitar, and bass – all made by himself, but he was so well liked, he never had to pay no fare on the train. He got his name from an old blues he was always singing.
>
> I hung around Old Man See-See Rider till I figured out how his guitar and fiddle were made. Then I went to the commissary and they give me a cigar box and big wooden box, and me and buddy name Louis mad a guitar out of the big box and I made a fiddle out of the cigar box. Then I went to

the woods and cut a hickory limb and I stole
thread from my mama to make the bow. Way we
got strings, me and Louis would go to the picnics
and barrelhouses and wait for See-See Rider to
break a string. We would tie them broken strings
together and put them on our homemade
instruments. And when See-See Rider seed I knew
how to play, he holp me fix the strings and
showed me some few tunes, so Louis and me
could play *Shortnin Bread* and *Old Hen Cackle* and
Uncle Bud.

We had to keep our instruments hid under the
house, because our mothers wanted us to be
preachers. We would go to church and when we
would come back, we would sneak under the
house and get our fiddle and guitar and then out
into the woods. The other children would follow
and we'd have a dance way out where their folks
couldn't find us.

One day the old folks had gone to town and all of
us kids got in the chicken house. We had killed
three of my mother's chickens and the girls were
cooking them. The kids were dancing while Louis
and me played *The Chicken Reel.* We had things
going good, but a white man heard us and walked
in on us. We both had got beatings from our
mothers about playing, but he just wanted to
know what we were playing and we told him See-
See Rider said it was a homemade fiddle. He
laughed and said, "Well, what's that on the fire?"

I didn't want to tell him, but he said not to be
scared because no one gonna bother us and he
told us to play some more. We played all three
pieces that we knew and he told us, "Bill, you and

Louis come with me," and we did. He taken us to his house and carried us out on the sun porch and called his wife and kids and some friends who was visiting his wife from town. Me and Louis was scared to death almost, and he said, "Boys, start playing just like you did in the hen house."

We started playing and I sang and all the white people and the cook and the handy man came in and started dancing and patting their hands. By that time it were dinnertime and he asked the cook what she had for dinner and she told him "baked ham." He said, "These boys like chicken," so she cooked us chicken and plenty of it. When we'd picked them chicken bones bare, he carried us home and lied for us – told our mother and father we had been cleaning up the commissary and paid us two dollars apiece. My mother told him, "You can work um any time." That white man laughed and said, "I will come by and get um again."

It was three or four weeks before we seen him again, but we would practice every time we got a chance. One day he came and got us and told us he had something for us. He sent to Sear and Rowback in Chicago and got us a brand-new fiddle and a guitar. We opened the box and got them out, but we couldn't play them. My homemade fiddle had only one string and the new one had four. He just laughed and told us to come every day and practice. I practiced for a long time till my brother-in-law showed me how to tune the fiddle. He could tune it, but he couldn't play it, and could play it but not tune it. So they used to pay him to tune and me to play. So I played for

those white peoples a long time and I also holp
my daddy raise cotton.

John Cephas

Homemade instruments were not confined to the
Mississippi Delta. Bluesman John Cephas recalled
growing up in the late 1930s and early 1940s in rural
Virginia:

> "Well, we used to take a wooden crate, like a box,
> a small wooden crate or a box – now I did this
> many times – and we'd put sticks on them and
> stuff like that, play a one-stringed guitar, or if we
> could get two strings of some kind attached to
> that. And we had all kinds of contraptions where
> you'd bend the neck to change the key or just slide
> something up and down it to change the note.
> Yeah, I used to do that."

Roy Clark

According to the *Hollywood Walk Of Fame Stardust*, Roy
Clark is born as the son of a tobacco farmer on April 15,
1933 in Meherrin, Virginia. Clark's first musical instrument
was a cigar box with a ukulele neck and four strings. His
father had rigged the musical box for him to play in an
elementary school band.

K. C. Douglas

Homemade instruments often suggest a special gift or
talent of the player. Here, rather than stressing rural
poverty, the makeshift instrument implies destiny. K. C.

Douglas of Canton, Mississippi, claims he used to beat on a water bucket until his fingers bled, trying to make it sound like a guitar. In retrospect, he considers his actions a sign that he was born to be a musician.

Sleepy John Estes

Blues legend Sleepy John Estes spoke of his experience and the importance of making a guitar to prove his worth as a musician to his mother.

> "Then I went and made me a cigar box with one string on it and start to playing it. The string come from a broom. You know, on a broom you had a wire wrapped around it to hold it. My mother told my father, said, 'That boy goin to be a musician, might as well buy him a guitar.' He said, 'Wait till fall and I'll buy you one.' So he worked and bought me that guitar."

Details of instrument construction, references to brooms, that the construction was viewed as a sign by his parents, their acceptance of the sign, and their willingness to sacrifice for his future emphasize John's inherent gift for music. He claims that even before this a seer determined he was going to be a musician: "When I was born, a man from Texas told my mother I was going to be a musician, said it was a talent."

Canray Fontenot

Canray Fontenot was born in 1922. He first learned music from his father, Adam, as Michael Doucet describes in his CD notes to Canray Fontenot:

Louisiana Hot Sauce Creole Style. [folkstreams.net >>
Dry Wood]

> Canray constructed his first violin at the age of
> nine. It was a cigar box with strings fashioned
> from a new screen door.... As Canray tells it,
> "Nonc Adam [Canray's father] was a hard man to
> please musically because you had to play
> everything so exact. One day I was playing my
> little fiddle behind the house when he turned the
> corner, stopped and asked me where did I get that
> contraption? I told him that I had made it myself.
> He was kind of shocked because I had always
> gone someplace alone when I was learning. But he
> assured me if I could play a tune he would get me
> a real fiddle. He must have liked the sounds,
> although I'm sure he was real surprised hearing a
> melody coming out of that cigar box! Anyway, he
> traded three dozen eggs and one sack of flour to
> Deo Langley, a real fine Indian fiddler, for a bright
> red fiddle. After about a year, I started sitting in
> with my father and Alphonse Lafleur, my old
> pop's fiddler, who really showed me how to
> second the accordion.

In "'If You Remember My Song, You'll Remember Me'
An Interview with Canray Fontenot" by Sharon Arms
Doucet (originally published in *Fiddler Magazine*, Fall
1995) which was conducted in June of that year, just
one month before Fontenot died of cancer, he spoke
again about the cigar box fiddle that he made himself.

> Yeah, a lot of people don't believe that. You see,
> my mama had a cousin who had a boy, Joe, that
> was a little older than me. We would go and play
> Douglas [Belair]'s fiddle when he wasn't around.

So all of a sudden, Douglas started being kind of famous, you know. They never had too many black fiddlers, you know. So Joe say, "Canray, we don't have no fiddle to practice on. We gonna make us some fiddles." I was about nine years old, I guess. So we got some cigar boxes and started working on that. I say, "Joe, where we gonna get some tools?" his older brother was a meat cutter. So Joe said, "Horace, he got a good knife. I'm pretty sure Saturday or Sunday he'll get drunk. I'm gonna steal his knife." So he stole his pocket knife, and we made our fiddles. Now after the fiddle was made, we took some wire from his mama's screen for strings, then we went in the woods and got some little switches that kind of looked like a bow. We took some sewing thread for the horsehair, and then we got our rosin from the pine tree.

So I'm try to play some tunes on my little fiddle. My mama's baby brother was older than me, and he would beat the triangle with my daddy. That was Joel [Victorien]. One day he came out and saw me. He say, "If you can start a tune on that thing there, I know darn well I can start a tune on a good fiddle. I'm gonna get me a fiddle." So he started shopping around, and he got himself a fiddle from Déo Langley, he's an Indian from Elton and he played the fiddle. He traded a bag of hulled rice and two dozen eggs for it. And in no time at all, my uncle was playing. So whenever he'd break a string, he'd give me the string. That would give some power to my fiddle. So we'd go wherever they had somebody playing the fiddle, and when they'd break a string, we'd pick it up. We had a pretty good sound then.

[The sewing thread on the bow,] oh, it was rough. But you knew what you was doing all the time. So my uncle got good in no time. So he went and bought a used fiddle, he paid fifteen dollars for that one. And he told me, "If you help me dig the sweet potatoes and stuff, I'll give you my little red fiddle." That's what I did. That's the first fiddle I ever had. But boy, it looked like that thing was long beside my cigar box. But I stayed with it. I never did have a real good fiddle.

Sharon Arms Doucet would later write *Fiddle Fever* in 2000 which shares a dedication "to the memory of Creole fiddler Canray Fontenot, who made his first fiddle from a cigar box." Set in 1914, *Fiddle Fever* is a tale of a young Félix LeBlanc who is captivated by the sweet sounds of the fiddle when his uncle comes to town. Doucet was inspired to write *Fiddle Fever* after hearing Fontenot's story.

Mance Lipscomb

Mance Lipscomb (April 9, 1895 – January 30, 1976) was an influential blues singer, guitarist and songster. Born Beau De Glen Lipscomb near Navasota, Texas, he as a youth took the name of 'Mance' from a friend of his oldest brother Charlie ("Mance" was short for "emancipation," a fitting moniker even though he was born after the Cavil War – perhaps he felt that music was his own form of emancipation). According to Paul Olivier in his work *Savannah Syncopators: African Retentions in the Blues*:

Mance Lipscomb's memories go back a few years longer (than 1901) and his family associates extend back into slavery. Mance's father was born a slave in Alabama. When still a boy, he and his [older] brother [Charlie] were separated from their parents and shipped to the newly settled Brazos bottoms of Texas. Then he made a fiddle out of a cigar box, and after... [Mance] became a full-time professional fiddler playing for dances...

Clyde "Judas" Maxwell

Mississippian Clyde "Judas" Maxwell considered homemade instruments incapable of producing real music. He recalled their construction as common practice but downplayed their importance to becoming a musician.

> A lot of em done that. But they didn't learn to play any music on it. Didn't play no music on it. Just some kind of noise. Now let's see, I used to have five... seven friends... and they make some kind of guitar out of them old buckets. They hit on an old bucket, puts tops on them and cuts holes in them – get strings. Put some strings on it and wind it up. But they never really learned hot to play it. They plunk it, everything else. But you think it sounds good, just plunk it and think you got a guitar. But it's not like a real one.

Kid Ory

Much about Kid Ory is a mystery. This snippet is taken from Nat Shapiro and Hentoff's *Hear Me Talkin' To Ya*, wherein the story of Kid Ory is told:

My first instrument was a cigar-box banjo that I made myself. When I was a little better than ten years old, my father bought me a real banjo from New Orleans. We used to go out on the bridge and practice. When I was thirteen, I formed a band where I lived then, in Laplace, Louisiana, about twenty-nine miles from New Orleans. We had a homemade violin, bass viol, guitar, banjo – played on a chair from drums. We saved all the money we made, except for fifteen cents a piece for carfare, so we could buy good instruments later. We used to go 'round crowds and hustle.

We saved the money and I decided to give picnics with beer, salad – fifteen cents to come in and dance. We played the same numbers we are playing now, like *Pallet on the Floor*, besides some waltzes. We used to go down to New Orleans week ends to hear the different bands that played in the parks. They play a tune once, that's all I want to hear so we could play it too. Take two and make one out of it if we couldn't get all of it.

Kid Ory makes an interesting statement in that he would borrow musical parts of songs and cobble those parts into something he could take away into a unique song of his own. Much like his homemade fiddle and banjo for his band, even his songs were put together out of what was available to him. All of this, to earn and save money for that cherished 'good' instrument to buy later.

ONE MAN'S TRASH

Carl Perkins

Quoted before the plans of a cigar box guitar in *Guitar Player* in 1976, Carl Perkins recalls:

> Before I went to school, I started fooling around on a guitar. My daddy made me one with a cigar box, a broomstick, and two strands of bailing wire and I'd sit and beat on that thing.

Eddie Taylor

Eddie Taylor speaks to the sound and being driven to play. Determined to learn to play the guitar any way he can, Taylor combines the gift and single-mindedness with the parental opposition and homemade guitar theme:

> "See, that's something born with you. Your mother and father can whip you to make you do what they want you to do. But you still are going to do what you want to do. Certain numbers they would play would stay in my mind. I used to go under the house and listen through the floor and hear that ringing in my head, and it wouldn't come out, and then I'd go and make me a guitar, with a cigar box and some broom wire. When a sound sticks in your head like that you can do it."

Eddie Taylor also spoke of instrument construction, like Sleepy John Estes opting for the broom:

> "I used to take my mama's broom and tear the wire off it and make me a guitar upside the wall – boom-boom-boom. The first real guitar I got was

in 1936. My mother ordered it from Sears Roebuck for twelve dollars."

Johnny Young

From Barry Lee Pearson's definitive work, *Sounds So Good To Me*, we learn about Johnny Young who was born New Year's Day 1917 (or 1918) in Vicksburg, Mississippi. Growing up in a musical family, his mother would host suppers, a type of down home house-rent party where the guests would buy food and drink and dance to the blues. Young's main influence was his uncle Anthony who was an accomplished musician on both guitar and violin, and it was Anthony who played at these suppers. By the age of twelve, Johnny Young was following in his uncle's footsteps.

> I'm from Vicksburg, Mississippi. My uncle was a professional musician. My mother blowed harmonica and my brother played harmonica, and I started when I was about eight years old. I made me a guitar out of a cigar box, and my mother say, "He's got to be a musician because he done made himself a guitar."

> So my mother said, "I got to buy him a guitar!" She bought me a five-dollar guitar, honest to God, she bought me a guitar and we used to play at home. And every night we had people come to listen to me play – you know, neighbors. And my brother was blowin the harmonica, you see, I was playin the guitar – Pat, we called him Pat – and my other brother had a broom. Now this was the act we had. He would look in the fireplace and get some ashes just like you got ashes to throw out,

put it on the floor. Whoop-de whoop-de, we had a bass goin.

And the people used to say, "Please let him play for my party tonight." My mama say, "He's too young, he's nothing, he's twelve years old."

Lost and Found

Through the course of my research, I have found many one line mentions of famous guitarists and other musicians who may be associated with an early start on a cigar box guitar. With some regret, I cannot do more than mention them here by name. The primary sources to back up their stories are unavailable or forgotten.

Louis Armstrong, George Benson, Scrapper Blackwell, Charlie Christian, Pee Wee Crayton, Albert Collins, Scott Dunbar, Buddy Guy, Jimi Hendrix, Lightnin Hopkins, Blind Willie Johnson, Albert King, Eddie Lang, King Bennie Nawahi, Fenton Robinson, Hound Dog Taylor, Josh White, and Robert Pete Williams.

Historic Cigar Box Instrument Plans

> *"He who works with his*
> *hands is a laborer,*
> *He who works with his*
> *hands and his head is an*
> *artisan,*
> *But he who works with his*
> *hands, his head, and his*
> *heart is an artist"*
>   - (attributed to) St.
>   Francis of Assisi

My first thought when assembling this chapter was that it would be convenient to have all of the plans for cigar box instruments in one place. What I didn't expect, after I had arranged them chronologically, was the striking difference from one set of plans to the next.

For example, the first set of plans written by Daniel Carter Beard, *How to Build an Uncle Enos Banjo*, gives details in near-Euclidean precision and encourages youngsters to use sharp pocketknives to whittle away the excess on cigar boxes and broom handles to create a banjo. As the plans become increasingly more contemporary, the use of tools is discouraged, and the instruments become oversimplified – eventually coming to the point where the cigar box guitar is no more than a set of rubber bands wrapped around the box with wooden spoon sticking out as a pretend neck.

While I can't say that any one technique or set of plans is more valid than the other, I am disturbed when I think that the target audience for the majority of these plans was intended for young boys and girls. Perhaps this is a comment on the way we educate our youth today. Or maybe a comment on the way our lives have changed over 150 years. To me, at least, it begs the question, is it so bad to consider a sharp pocketknife in the hands of a 10-year-old?

As a young Boy Scout I certainly had my share of accidents with a pocketknife. Most of my injuries were minor, and I think I only cut myself badly enough to receive stitches on one occasion, but these are the experiences that life is made up of. I suppose it comes as no coincidence then that my work with a pocketknife and its relation to being a Boy Scout brings me closer to the thinking of Daniel Carter Beard: rather than strive to protect youngsters from injury, there is value in being a little savage and dangerous and to risk injury for the sake of educating ourselves. I am far more troubled by the thought of an empty cigar box wrapped with rubber bands in the hands of a future musician, and to call such a contraption a cigar box guitar.

As you read through the plans for making cigar box instruments, you may draw a different conclusion.

1884 – Uncle Enos Cigar Box Banjo

Daniel C Beard published "Christmas Eve with Uncle Enos," in *The Book Buyer Christmas Annual* [A Summary of American and Foreign Literature, New York, Nov/Dec 1884, pp 311-314] which included plans to build an Uncle Enos Banjo.

> Tom, Dick, and Harry were sitting around a big, blazing wood fire in a log farmhouse of Christmas morning, when their attention was attracted by the shuffling of feet and the thumping of a banjo.

> "I thought Uncle Enos had broken his banjo," said one of the boys, after all three had listened for some time to the jollity going on among the colored people.

> "That he did," answered another; "or, rather, it all went to pieces, like the one-horse chaise."

"You know," he continued, "the instrument was made of a big bottle-gourd, and the dry weather last summer cracked it all apart."

"Harry," exclaimed Tom, "listen! That's no gourd instrument; no sir-ree! It has much too fine a tone. I tell you, fellers, I'm going out to take a look."

Upon the boy's meeting with Uncle Enos, he reveals his new instrument.

"He'a my banjo, Massa Tom," said the old man, displaying the musical instrument."
"Give us a tune, uncle, please," cried all the boys together, "and we will look at the banjo afterward."

After hearing Uncle Enos tune the banjo and start to play, the three boys are captivated by the "irresistibly contagious negro melody." The three boys examine the banjo briefly, "Well, I do declare!" cried Harry, "if uncle has not made it of a cigar-box, a broomstick, a bit of an old shoe, and a piece of clapboard!" Beard continues on a tangent after this point and diverts the reader to a large Christmas pudding where each would take turns putting their hands into the plum pudding and pulling out the first trinket they touched. Uncle Enos, incidentally, extracts a pair of gum shoes and a cold baked opossum – "gaily decked with ribbons and rosettes."

After these festive performances, the boys called Uncle Enos again to examine the wonderful banjo. Harry was right: there was not only a sweet tone to the instrument, but real melody when the hard fingers of the good old "darky" picked the strings.

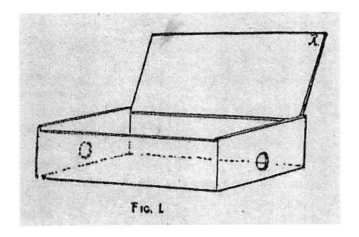

Fig. No. 1 shows the cigar-box, with holes bored through the ends for the stick that supports the neck to pass through. The bottom of the box is used for the top to the banjo. The lid of the box may be left on, so that it can be closed or opened, as the taste or ear of the banjoist may direct.

Fig. No. 2 represents a pine board with a plan of the neck drawn upon it, ready to be sawed out. d, d', d", d''' mark the spots where holes are to bored through for the key to turn in. The place for the low bridge that separates the strings before they enter the key is marked by the dotted lines at "a"; a rectangular slot should be cut here to fit the bridge (Fig. 5) into, as shown by the side-view of the neck (Fig. 9); b (Fig. 2) is a key hole in the side of the neck for the short string. See side-view (Fig. 9).

The slot for a small bridge for the short string of the banjo is marked by the dotted lines at c (Fig. 2). This little bridge is fitted in the slot, as shown in the side-view (Fig. 9).

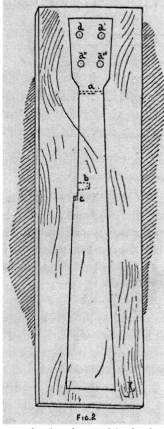

Fig. 3 shows the broomstick, whittled down at one end, so as to fit the holes bored in the cigar-box, through which it must pass and protrude about one-half inch at the butt. The top to the upper part of the broomstick is smoothed off flat, so that the neck (Fig. 2) may be securely screwed on to it, as is more clearly shown by the side-view (Fig. 9).

Fig. 4 shows what shape to make the keys. The latter must have holes (just large enough for the banjo strings to pass through) bored near the ends, as shown by the diagram. The keys may be made of any kind of wood – hard wood is the best.

Fig. 5 shows the bridge that fits into the slot a (Fig. 2) already described.

Fig. 6 is simply a piece of tin bent into the shape shown in the diagram, and made to fit over the butt-end of the banjo for the wires of Fig. 7 to pass over when the latter is put in place (see Fig. 10).

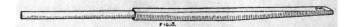

Fig. 7 is a piece of hard wood (Uncle Enos used leather), with five small holes bored through it for the attachment of the banjo strings, and a wire loop at the end that passes over the piece of tin (Fig. 6) and is held in place by the tension of the strings and the protruding end of the broomstick at the butt of the banjo (Fig. 10).

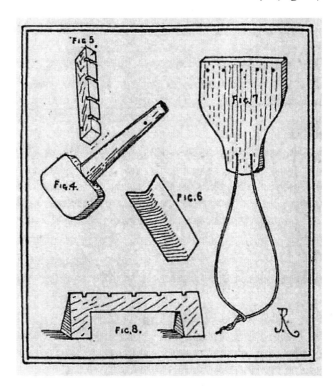

The bridge proper is shown by Fig. 8. It may be cut from a piece of soft pine in a few moments with a pocket-knife. Its place is in front of Fig. 7, where it spreads the five strings before they pass over the head and neck of the instrument.

Fig. 9 shows the neck finished and all ready to be fitted to the box. The neck is fastened to its broomstick support by two screws, as may be seen in the diagram.

Fig. 10 shows the finished instrument, all strung and ready for use.

Fig. 11 shows the arrangement of the banjo strings. The shortest string on a banjo is the 5th. And now we have reached the part where the boy who wants to make an Uncle Enos banjo will have to expend a few cents. Go to a dealer, and for the 1st and 5th ask for E strings. Let the first be a little heavier than the 5th. The 2nd should also be an E string, but much heavier than the 1st. for the 3rd, ask for a guitar B string. The 4th, or bass string, is manufactured especially for the now popular banjo, and care must be taken not to purchase the guitar D for the banjo A, or bass; both strings are silver, wound on silk, but the latter is much finer wound than the guitar D.

Harry, who is said by Tom and Dick to have a musical ear, made a banjo under the direction of his old friend Uncle Enos, and he says the whole thing cost him but half a day's labor and forty cents for strings.

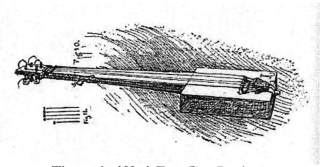

The completed Uncle Enos Cigar Box banjo

Tailpiece at the end of Christmas Eve With Uncle Enos, showing gum shoes in plum pudding

1886 – John Richards Cigar Box Banjo

Originally published in *Harpers Young People (Vol VII, Feb 23, 1886 pp262-263)*, John Richards gives plans very similar to the Uncle Enos Banjo featured in Beard's book. Copies of these plans are also published in the March 25, 1886, Waterloo, edition of the *Iowa State Reporter* in that same year with credit given to John Richards and Harpers Young People.

A Cigar-Box banjo is something which most boys have heard of, and some have attempted, with more or less success, to make. Possibly their older relatives have ridiculed the home-made instrument, and it has had to contend against prejudice, which, as we know, is almost fatal to success. Nevertheless such a banjo, if carefully made and properly strung, can be made to give forth very musical tones, and where the "real thing" cannot be had, the combination of cigar box and broomstick makes a good substitute. If you would like to try your hands at it, I will tell you how to go to work.

Procure a cigar box eight and a quarter inches long, four and three-quarter inches wide, and two and a quarter inches deep. This is the ordinary size of a box used to contain fifty cigars.

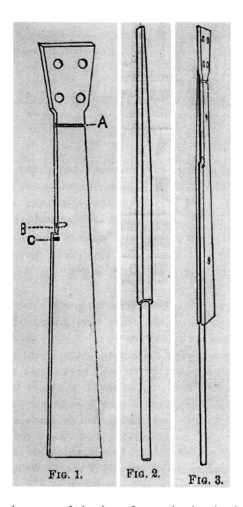

Fig. 1.   Fig. 2.   Fig. 3.

The bottom of the box forms the head of the banjo, thus allowing the cover to be opened or shut. In each end of the box cut two round holes, three-quarters of an inch in diameter, half an inch from the top and an equal distance from the two sides of the box.

With a lead-pencil mark off, on a piece of soft wood nineteen inches long, four inches wide, and half an inch thick, the shape of the handle as shown in Fig. 1. Before sawing the handle out, the four key-holes should be bored, each hole being a quarter of an inch in diameter. Then shape the handle according to the outline of the diagram, and across the top of the handle cut a groove three-sixteenths of an inch wide and equally deep (A, Fig. 1); this is to hold a small bridge to keep the strings from touching the handle.

In the side of the handle drill a hole half an inch above the angle (B, Fig. 1) – this is to hold the fifth key; and just below the angle a groove three-sixteenths of an inch wide and equally deep should be cut for the purpose of holding a small bridge for the fifth string (C, Fig. 1).

Fig. 4.

From an old broom cut a piece of stick twenty-four inches long; whittle this flat on one side, and on the other side, eight inches from the end, cut the stick away so that it will slope and become flat at the end (Fig. 2). Eight and three-quarter inches of the other end of the stick must be cut away, so as to fit snugly the holes in the cigar box, the end projecting slightly. This broomstick is the backbone of the handle, which is fastened to it by two three-quarter-inch screws, as shown in Fig. 3.

Five keys shaped like Fig. 4 can be cut out of tough pieces of wood, each piece being half an inch thick, two and a quarter inches long, and one inch wide. Make those belonging to the key-board fit tightly in their holes. The key for the fifth string can be cut half an inch shorter than the others. Each key should have a hole bored through it, as shown in Fig. 4.

The small bridge is a piece of wood a quarter of an inch high and three-sixteenths of an inch wide, which is made to fit the groove (Fig. 1, A), with four notches cut in to conduct the strings. A similar bridge, with only one notch, and a quarter of an inch long, will answer for the fifth string.

The large bridge is made of a piece of wood two inches long, five-eights of and inch wide, and a quarter of an inch thick. The shape of

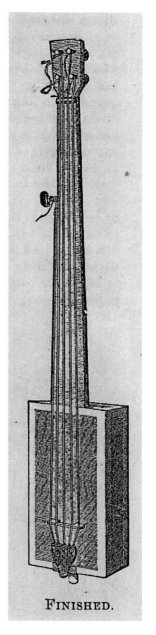

FINISHED.

the bridge can be seen in the illustration of the finished banjo. Five notches an equal distance from each other should then be cut in the top edge of the bridge.

The tail-piece is the piece to which the strings are attached at the lower end of the instrument. It is made from a piece of hard wood an inch and a half long, an inch and a quarter wide, and a quarter of an inch thick. Five small holes an equal distance apart and a quarter of an inch from the end of the piece of wood must first be drilled, and through the small end two holes a quarter of an inch apart and three-eighths of an inch from the end should be drilled to allow a piece of wire about six inches in length to pass through them. A piece of tin an inch and a quarter long and three-quarters of an inch wide, bent so as to fit on the edge of the box, will be required. Strings can be purchased at almost any music store.

Having purchased the strings, begin to put the various parts together by fitting the handle through the holes in the cigar box and the small bridges in their respective grooves. The tail-piece is then fastened close to the end of the box by twisting the wire around the projecting piece of broomstick and staying it. Place the piece of bent tin on the edge of the box under the wire holding the tail-piece, thus preventing the wire from damaging the box. Fit the keys in the key-board and the short key into the hole in the side of the handle. Knot the strings before threading them through the holes in the tail-piece. Before tightening the strings the last bridge is placed under the strings, two and a half inches from the end of the box, and your banjo is finished.

1912 – Cigar Box Zither

HOW TO MAKE DOOR ZITHER FROM CIGAR BOX

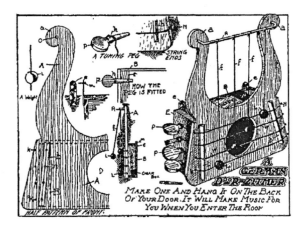

Here is an idea from Germany for those boys who are musically inclined, and who want to know how to make something to interest the whole family. The Germans call it a "Thur-zither" — at least that is the way they pronounce it — and it consists of a suitable sound box, B. with strings tuned to some minor chord of music, stretched over a hole at one side.

A framework above holds a crossbar, R, and from this hang threads with lead balls on the ends, arranged so that there is a ball opposite every wire string.

This instrument is hung on the back of the door of your room. When anyone comes in the movement of the opening door starts the balls to swinging on the ends of their cords, and as they swing they hit the wire strings.

Thus, acting as the hammers of a piano, they tap out the notes of the tuned strings so that there comes to one; faintly and as music from a long distance away the sound of the chords to which the strings are tuned, sweet and clear at first and gradually dying away to nothing as the vibration of the lead balls ceases. If carefully made the music is delightful and the whole arrangement can be made very decorative, an ornament for any room, and a novelty which will always be an enjoyment. Commonly seen in Germany, through the toy districts around Stuttgart, Nuremberg, etc., the idea, is too good to leave to foreign countries alone, so we will get to work and make one for ourselves.

CIGAR BOX BASIS OF WORK

The sound box we will not bother to make ourselves, for it must be of thin wood, carefully fitted and evenly shaped, and when we can find a cigar box already done for us in this manner we might as well use it as to take our own time, since the size and shape will do very well for our purpose.

If you want an especially fine tone, however, or want to make a bigger one you can build up the box in your own way with glued joints and all, or take the cigar box to pieces and put it together with glue in the joints, making every crack airtight. This will, improve the tone of the instrument considerably. This cigar box part is shown at B in the drawings, the whole box being used with the exception of the cover.

In place of the cover of the box we fit on a front piece made of thin wood as at A in the drawings. This is shaped as shown, with two arms reaching up above to support a cross bar (R), from which the strings will hang with the balls, L, at the lower: end.

This front piece is cut to pattern, half of which is shown in the drawing at the left. Enlarge this to a size so that the cigar box will fit in at the back of the lower part, as shown by the dotted lines in the pattern drawing.

The upper part curves in and out in two arms, one on either side, the total width at the top being a little less than the bottom width. The slanting out of the lower part is merely to add to the appearance of the device when done.

In the center of this lower part cut the hole shown, this being about half as big across as the front of your cigar box.

The rounded parts (a) at the top of the side arms of A have small holes at O from which runs the wire cross bar, R, arranged as shown.

ONE MAN'S TRASH

WOODEN CROSS BAR WILL DO

A wooden cross bar will do just as well as a metal one if you haven't the wire handy, and this can be fastened on with small brads or glue. It should stick out about a half an inch beyond the face of the front piece, A.

At the end of the cigar box a half inch piece (E) is fitted. This can be fitted inside. If you are working for better appearance of the finished instrument, or outside if you want greater volume in the sound box. It is shown outside in the assembled drawing at the right, and inside in the small detail in the center, showing how the pegs are fitted, but either way will do.

This piece should be fastened on securely and glued if you have glue handy.

Bore four holes in it for the pegs (P) each a quarter of an inch in diameter and running through the piece E and the box end. Space them an inch apart and along the center line of the end side in — take the handle end of a file when the holes are bored — from out and using it as a reamer, twisting it in the holes, ream them out tapered so that they are bigger at the outer end than inside as in the separate drawing showing the peg P fitting the tapered hole as shown.

Drill four small holes (K) through A where the edge of the cigar box comes at the "peg" end of the box, these spaced three-quarters of an inch apart. At the other end at N drive four small nails equally spaced and opposite. The strings W will stretch between these over bridges (b) as shown.

Theses bridges are three contoured strips of hard-wood say a quarter of an inch high, with little notches at the top where the strings cross spaced three-quarters of an inch apart also.

BANJO STRINGS FOR WIRES

Use steel banjo strings for the wires and, tying them to the nails, N, run them across the bridges, which, are glued in place, down through the holes (k) and to the holes (h) in the pegs P, which fit the tapered holes in E.

The drawings show how these pegs are cut, made of hard or soft wood, but tapered like the holes in E. The wires pass through small holes (h) in the shank of the peg, so that when the peg is turned the wire is wound up on the shank. When tight a shove in will wedge the peg tightly in its hole so it can't slip back and get the wire, out of tune.

Thus the pegs are used to tune the wires to whatever chord you want.

Do not make the handle part of the pegs too big or they will interfere with each other in turning. Three-quarters of an inch wide is enough.

Now you are ready to hang the hammer balls L. These are nothing but large split lead shot, nearly a half inch in diameter, and can be obtained at any fishing: tackle store. Fasten those to silk threads as you would to a fish line and tie them hanging from the cross bar R, each. cord being of a length so that a ball will hang directly opposite each wire

W. Space them evenly all along the bar R. as shown

At the back of the cigar box B tack tin pieces as at (e) in the drawings with a hole in each, to hang the instrument by.

This done, varnish the whole thing and let it dry. A couple of coats of shellac varnish will do well — costs ten cents — and then you are ready to hang it on the back of your door and amuse the visitors in guessing where the music comes from.

"Thur-zither" is more than a toy and will repay any one for the making, but make it with cure, so that when done you can be proud of the workmanship as well as the idea.

1919 – Cigar Box Ukulele

As written by S. H. Samuels in *The Boy Mechanic Book 3: 800 Things for a Boy to Do*. [Popular Mechanics, Chicago, 1919, Page 358]

A Homemade Hawaiian Ukulele
By S. H. Samuels

The one-string banjo, the cigar box guitar, and similar vaudeville favorites are giving way to the tantalizing ukulele, and the home mechanic, to be up to date in his musical craftsmanship, must fall in line. The size of this instrument makes it especially suited to the cigar-box type of body construction, as detailed in the several sketches and shown in the photograph reproduced. This neat ukulele was made at a cost of 30 cents by careful selection of materials from the shop scrap stock.

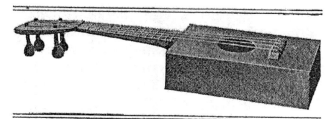

This Cigar-Box Ukulele cost the maker 30 cents, and affords him the pleasures of a more expensive one

A cigar box of good quality Spanish cedar, about 2-1/2 x 6 x 6 in., as shown in Fig 1 is used for the body. Remove the paper carefully, so as not to mar the surface, soaking it if necessary. Take it apart, and if the nail holes are too numerous, or broken out, trim off the edges. Fit the parts of the body together, as shown in Fig 2, the top and bottom pieces resting against the side and end pieces, and the latter between the sides. Cut the 2-1/2 in. hole in the top piece as shown, 3-3/4 in. from the neck end. To reinforce the body make strips A, 1/4 in. square, and fit them to be glued into the corners at the top and bottom. Make strips B, 1/4 by 5/8 by 4-1/2 in., and glue them under the top and on the bottom as indicated in Fig 2. The final assembling and gluing of these parts, using animal glue, should be done after the bridge C is in place, and the other parts are made. The bridge is of hard wood hollowed underneath the notched edge, as detailed, and is fitted with a metal string contact.

Spanish cedar or mahogany is suitable for the neck, detailed in Fig 3. A single piece is best, but the extension for the pegs and the wider end at the body may be joined and glued to the main portion of the neck. Dowels should then be used to reinforce the joints. The outline of the parts of the neck are shown in detail in Fig 3. In the sectional view at the right, the shape of the neck at the thinnest and thickest parts is shown by the two upper curved, dotted lines. The nut D is made of mahogany, walnut, or other hard wood, the grain extending lengthwise, and the notches for the strings spaced as shown.

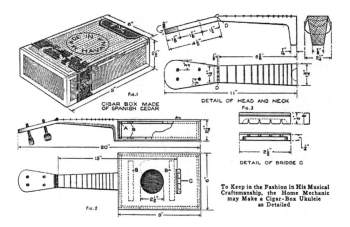

DETAIL OF HEAD AND NECK
Fig.3

CIGAR BOX MADE
OF SPANISH CEDAR

Fig.1

Fig.2

DETAIL OF BRIDGE C

To Keep in the Fashion in His Musical
Craftsmanship, the Home Mechanic
may Make a Cigar-Box Ukulele
as Detailed

The making and spacing of the frets must be done very carefully. They are of aluminum, brass and other metals being suitable also. Make the frets 1/16 by 3/16 in. and cut grooves 1/8 in. deep for them. The spacing of the frets is determined as follows, a standard practice: The distance from the metal string-contact on the bridge to the nut should be measured carefully. The first fret, near the head, is 1/18 of this distance from the nut, the total length being in this instance 13 in. The second fret is set 1/18 the distance from the first fret to the bridge; the third, 1/18 from the second fret to the bridge, etc. The frets must fit tightly in the grooves, requiring no special fastening. The tuning pegs may be bought or made.

In assembling the parts, fasten the end of the body to the neck, with glue, reinforced by screws. Set its upper edge parallel with the fingerboard, and so that the latter is flush with the top of the body, when fitted to it. Assemble the body, without the top, gluing it to the end, fixed to the neck. When this portion is thoroughly dried, fit the top into place finally, and glue it. The whole

253

construction is then cleaned, sandpapered, stained, and shellacked or varnished. The stringing of the instrument is simple, and the strings may be purchased in sets.

1920 – How to Make a Jazzolin from a Broomstick

In July 1920 *Popular Science* publishes How to Make a Jazzolin from a Broomstick, by Frank Vroom.

This instrument is a source of great amusement to the music lover and is one that can be easily played by anyone as it embodies only one string.

Frets or marks may be made at the proper intervals on the fingerboard to guide the novice on placing his fingers. They may be copied from those on a guitar or mandolin or made by finding the scale on the instrument itself.

The body consists of a small-sized cigar box, the front cover cut as shown in the illustration, measuring 1 ¾ in. from each corner and 2 ½ in. down on the sides.

The sound holes are shaped like the warrior club, or the conventional F hole may be substituted, the length being 3 in., the width 3/16 in. on one end and widening to 3/8 in. on the other. Set them in or on an angle as shown, 1 ½ in. in on front and ½ in. on the back. The side view gives the position of the inside blocks – front and back – that in front being 1 ¼ by 1 ¼ by 2 ¼ in. while the back one is ½ by ½ by 1 ¾ in. the height will vary according to the depth of the box.

Here is the way the jazzolin will appear when finished. Anyone can play it with but little practice

Bevel the top of the front block 1/8 of an in. to form the slant for the fingerboard. Bore holes in the back of the block for the button peg. Clamp the broom handle in a vise and plane off the top until the width is a trifle over ½ in. now measure in 4 in. on one end, and down ¼ in. from the 4 in. mark, cutting out with a fret saw. The length of the whole will be 15 in. now measure in 1 ¾ in. from the other end and drill holes ¾ in. the depth of the handle, 7/16 in. wide and 1 ¼ in. long. A small strip of bone is fastened upon this end as well as one on the back of the box. These should have small grooves filed in the center of the top for the string. The key is made from hardwood and must taper like a violin key. The design may be varied to suit the ideas of the builder.

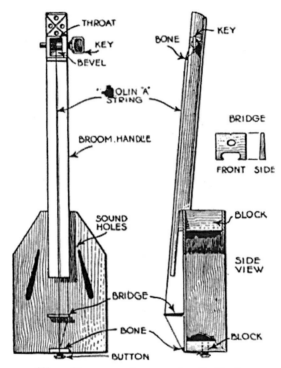

The diagram above sets forth in detail every part of the construction and you should encounter no difficulty in making the instrument

The design on the end is made with a three-cornered file and a small drill. The bridge is 1 in. in height and 1 ¼ in. wide. Cut in ¼ in. on the bottom to form the feet. Taper the thickness of the height from 3/16 in. to 1/8 in.

Make a small peg and insert it in the rear block. Glue strips on the top inside edges and after fastening the fingerboard through the front block set in the top and glue it securely. Now bore a hole through the top of the finger board into the block, and countersink the screw which holds it. If desired the bridge may be rounded slightly on the top while the two pegs are made for the front and back. This will allow the use of two strings tuned in fifths or five tones between their pitches, preferably E and A violin strings. Use only silk or gut strings as a steel string will sound much too tinny. Cut the grooves for the strings about 3/8 in. deep – if more than one is to be used. This will allow plenty of drop for the bow.

Purchase a cheap bow from some music store or pawn shop but be sure that the hair is in good condition, and it should be kept well rosined. Decorate the edges and corners of the instrument with narrow strips of colored paper and give it two coats of white shellac, rubbing down the fingerboard after each coat.

For a more finished instrument a hole can be bored in the back block under the peg, and in it a round stick about 25 in. in length may be inserted to give a substantial rest for the instrument. When finished this way it resembles the 'cello.

The jazzolin somewhat resembles the ukulele except for the fact that it is played with a violin bow instead of a pick. Several of these instruments in conjunction with a piano will render very pleasing music. The popular "jazz" music becomes easy, once one is accustomed to using the bow.

1921 – One String Cigar Box Fiddle

On June 24, 1921, *The Sandusky Star Journal* claims:

CIGAR BOX FIDDLES ARE EASY TO MAKE

While a cigar box fiddle does not make the sweetest and best music in the world it is entertaining and has been used successfully for that purpose on the stage and in homes, many many times. To make one, first get an old cigar box. Take the paper off it, and pull off the lid. Plane a three foot broom handle in half. Smooth down the flat side with your knife and some sandpaper. In the top end of the stick, about two inches down, bore a small hole to receive a peg to which the string of the fiddle, which should be a "D" violin string, is fastened. Cut a long notch in the other end of the stick so the lid of the cigar box fits on snugly and smoothly. The broom stick need extend only about half way along the length of the lid, as shown by the dotted lines in the illustration. Fasten the lid to the stick with brads. Center it on the broom handle. Be careful not to crack it. In each side of the lid, using a sharp jackknife, cut two "S" shaped holes, similar to those in a real violin. These slots should be about three inches long and the cut should be one quarter of an inch wide.

Before fastening the lid to the box, cut a groove in the end of it to receive the rounded side of the broomstick. Then carefully tack on the lid. In the bottom end of the box, directly in line with the end of the broom stick, bore a small hole into which another peg, this one about a half an inch long, is snuggly fitted. Fasten the other end of the fiddle string to this peg. A hand-made bridge to hold the string up should be placed on the lid of the box. It need not be glued or tacked. All this done, the fiddle is ready for tuning. Tune it up to any note on the piano. A regular violin bow may be used in playing.

1922 – Cigar Box Mandolin

Ironically, the cigar box mandolin is very rare in both construction and plans. The irony comes from the fact that the mandolin, traditionally, was relegated to the youngest member of the family to play. With the stigma of cigar box guitars as toys or beginner instruments for children being so prevalent throughout the history of the instrument, why then are there not more cigar box mandolins?

From *The Charleston Daily Mail*, March 24, 1922

FOR THE YOUNG PEOPLE

No one can compute the energy which has been wasted in the vain endeavor to make a playable instrument of the mandolin type with a cigar box as the basis of inspiration, but the writer recalls one which was made, by a "Handy Boy" while he was convalescing from a long illness, and he will endeavor to tell the story of its making here.

The first thing was to find a perfect cigar box, with no splits nor broken pieces; it was taken apart carefully to be sure the delicate wood was not split in the process. The paper was scraped off and the joints of the box glued and nailed together again, excepting the top, which was left off to allow the small glue blocks e and f to be glued in place by spreading glue on two sides of the block and rubbing it into perfect contact with the angle. These glue blocks were about 1/2" across the long angle and not more than 5/8" long and were glued into all corners and around the inside of the top edge of the sides as at f; after the glue was thoroughly hardened those at f were planed off to receive the top later. The neck was whittled from a piece of soft white wood or poplar, and the dowel g of the neck fitted to the box by boring 3/4" holes through the ends of the box to receive it, glued in its place, and nailed through the end of the box into the neck where they joined. The bass bar d was made and glued on the under side of the top as at d after which the 2" hole was cut in the top and the sounding post 1/4" in diameter, Just enough higher than the sides to stay in place was glued upright on the bottom. When this had set, the top was glued on the sides and glue blocks f, and a weight placed upon it until the next day when the glue had thoroughly hardened. The box was then carefully smoothed and sandpapered; the nut, saddle and bridge were whittled from maple and glued in their places; note that the neck is cut below the finger board to receive the nut at a, and that the fingerboard projects above the box where they are joined. The pegs with tapered shafts were whittled from maple and the 5/16" holes in the head were tapered with a round file to receive them.

This handy boy used old violin strings, but strings of various sizes may be made of wire, of hard fish line or of varying numbers of strands of fine silk; these fish lines and silk strings may be shellaced and allowed to become thoroughly hard.

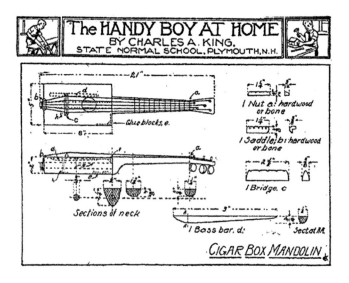

The most difficult thing is the placing of the frets in the fingerboard, which regulate the fingering, and the pitch of the string. The frets may be made of a piece of tin about. [illegible]" wide, doubled over to make the top edge round so it will not cut the string, and fitted into a fine saw cut made 1/8" deep which must be so placed as to make the correct tone. The best way to do this is to string the instrument, and by moving a piece of wire back and forth find the correct location by comparing the tone with, a piano or other instrument of correct tone. Make every tone and half tone for an octave, the octaves first, then the fifth, the thirds, the tones and the half tones. Such an instrument may have from four to eight strings, or may have five [sic] double strings as in a standard mandolin. It may be played with the fingers, or with a plectrum or picker, which may be made of a discarded tortoise shell comb. After the frets have been glued in their places, the instrument was unstrung and given a coat of dark mahogany stain, followed by two coats of hard varnish.

1922 – Cigar Box Ukulele

First appearing in the *Aunt Elsie Magazine* of *The Oakland Tribune*, October 8, 1922, and then again (with some corrections in spelling) in *The Janesville Daily Gazette*, January 25, 1923, Lewis Allen Brown writes:

ADVENTURE TRAILS
BLAZED FOR YOU

A few raindrops splattered down on the camp and Ted dashed out and secured a cigar box that had been drying in the sun for several days. He thrust it under his coat as he dashed back. It was a cigar box he had secured at the store, and from which he had soaked of all the labels and other paper.

"You'd think that was valuable," laughed Ned.

"Don't want it to get wet, can't make a good 'Boxelele' out of it," explained Ted.

"Whoever heard of a 'boxelele.'" laughed Ned.

"It's a word I invented and by good rights it should be" 'cigar-boxelele' - it means a sort of ukelele made out of a cigar box."

"Aw, you can't make a uke out of a cigar box—"

"I can try," laughed Ted, "and as it looks like a steady rain I might start in now."

Ned was promptly interested. He watched Ted to get out glue, wires, screws and other things but at the same time he laughed, as he didn't believe Ted could really make a musical instrument out of it.

"If you get a real cedar sigar box like this," said Ted, "and not a cheap imitation cedar box, or a white-wood box veneered with cedar, you can get some fine vibrations out of it."

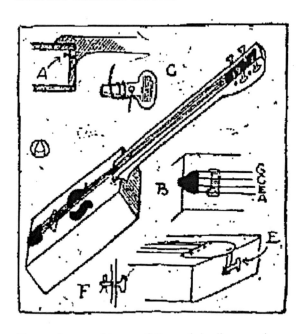

He sandpapered it, carefully took it all apart, threw away the nails and glued it together, after he had first cut the funny, crooked sound holes.

"The violin-shaped sound holes are better than the big round one with a cigar box," he explained.

The string arm he also fastened on with a screw and glue before fastening on the bottom, as shown at (A1). Then he put in the string peg also before putting on the bottom. Arrow at (E) shows the string peg and (F) shows how it is fastened with a home-made wire cotter pin. After that he bound it around and around tightly with cord and wrapped it in a blanket to keep it out of the damp air.

"Now," said Ted. "let's put on our bathing suits and go catch some catfish—it's just the weather— unless it thunders." He had learned that catfish would not bite when it thundered.

"But your 'boxelele' thing—" began Ned.

"Glue's got to harden a week," Ted told him, and so they went fishing.

It was more than a week later before Ted got a chance to finish his home-made ukelele. He sandpapered it again, over and over, varnished it over with shellac, cut out or mortised the peg place as the drawing shows (X) made and perforated the pegs (C) and dug up the old strings he had written home for. The pegs are rounded and tapered, so that by pushing in as you turn, to tune, they stick where ever you want them.

The drawing shows the little bridge, (E) shows how the tailpiece, of thin hard-wood, is perforated and fastened on and (B) shows the position of the strings. Some ukeleles use different strings, including F sharp, but the G-C-E-A arrangement is simplest and best.

Then; with a tuning fork Ted got "A" and tuned the other strings to match and he was ready.

"Plinkey-plink-e-plunk." went Ted.

"Well, what do you know—it does play!" exclaimed Ned, and he was quite right.

Make one for yourself—it's not difficult, and you'll be surprised to hear what a really sweet tone it has.

1923 – Musical Instruments from Cigar Boxes

In September 1923, *Popular Mechanics* published this article on Musical Instruments from Cigar Boxes by W. F. Cord.

> Cigar boxes, which may generally be obtained for the asking from and tobacconist – who will be glad to get rid of them – can be used to make very passable violins and mandolins. Of course, it is not expected that a "fiddle" of this variety would possess the tone of a Cremona or Stradivarius, but, in the hands of one knowing how to play such an instrument, very creditable results may be attained.
>
> The drawing shows the dimensions and appearances of the various necks in case it is desired to make them at home. However, if the best results are desired, it is recommended that these, as well as the bridges, tailpieces, strings, and similar fittings, be purchased from a music-supply house. If made at home, poplar should be used.
>
> The cigar-box violin should be made from a box about 3 in. deep, 5 in. wide, and from 9 ½ to 12 in. long, according to the person for whom it is made. Let the lid form the back of the instrument,

but do not nail it down until the work has been completed. Glue a block, 3/8 in. wide by 2 ½ in. long and the same depth as the box, in the end to which the neck is to be fastened, and a smaller block at the opposite end. Cut the F-shaped sound holes in the top and then drive in a few more nails around the edges of the box, to make it stronger. When the neck has been completed, drill two or three holes through the block and box into the neck for screws; then glue the neck in place, and screw it on tight. Next fasten the fingerboard in place, drill a hole in the rear end and rear block, and glue into it a small peg to hold the tailpiece. The bow is also made of poplar, and the hairs can be obtained from a long-tailed horse or bought from a music store; ordinary thread can even be used, where it is not possible to obtain horse-hair, or to purchase a bow.

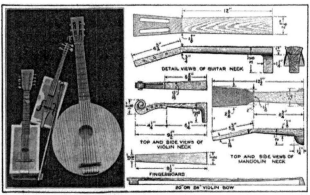

Violin, Mandolin, and Guitar That are Made from Cigar and Cheese Boxes by the Addition of Suitable Necks and Fittings; Anyone Who can Play a Standard Instrument of Either Kind can Produce Music from These

For the mandolin, a box about 5 ½ or 6 in. wide, 2 ¾ to 3 ¾ in. deep, and 9 ½ in. long, will be best. The lid, as in the violin, forms the back and is not fastened down until the remainder of the work is done. The sound hole, which is about at the center of the box, is 1 ¼ by 1 ¾ in. in size. Glue a piece of wood, ¼ by 5/8 in. in dimensions, across the box, midway between the sound hold and the end of the box, to keep the bridge and finger board from pressing in the top. A block, 3/8 in. wide by 3 in. long, and the same height as the box, is glued inside at the neck end. The neck is made as indicated in the drawing, and is attached to the box as described for the violin.

The guitar is made from part of a cheese box instead of a cigar box. A box made from a single piece of wood, instead of one made up from three-ply veneer, should be selected. Cut the rim down to 3 ¼ in. in width, and attach the neck at the point where the ends meet, after fastening a ¾ by 3 ¼ by 3 ¼ in. block on the inside. The neck, when in place, must stand above the rim a sufficient distance so that, when the top is applied, the neck will be flush with the top. After the neck has been fitted, as described above, the top and bottom can be put on; these pieces may be sawed from pine, poplar or almost any kind of lumber, about 1/8 in. thick. The sound hole is a little above the center and is 2 ¾ in. in diameter. The top is glued and nailed to the rim and is reinforced by three ¼ by 5/8 in. strips that are glued edgewise across the underside of the top to prevent it from being pressed in. It is also advisable to glue two or three such strips on the bottom before it is attached. A lug, 1 ¼ in. long by 1 ½ in. wide, is left on the bottom cover, and fastened to the underside of the neck.

1931 – Cigar Box Uke

In *Comfort Magazine*, October 1931, a set of plans for a cigar box uke are published. They are similar to a set of plans to his cigar box mandolin in 1922.

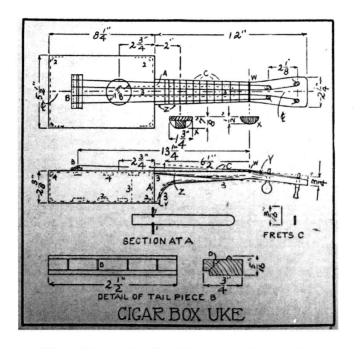

CIGAR BOX UKE

What "Handy Boy" with an ear for tinkling sounds has not tried to make something of this sort? It was not a success in every case, but any

273

one who can use the simple tools may safely venture to make this instrument.

Secure a good cigar box of about the dimensions given; moisten the paper around the corners and tear and scrape off as much as possible, sandpapering the rest after the box had dried. Nail the corners of the sides, ends and bottom, and glue corner blocks as at 2, leaving the top until later. Make a ¾ inch neck 3 the width of the inside of the box and 8 inches long; cut grooves to receive the end of the box as shown and cut a piece out of the end as at A1 to fin into these grooves. Fit the pieces but do not fasten at this time. Make the ginger-board and head pieces ¾ inches x 2 ¼ inches x 12 inches. Plane the finger-board at Z and the top side of the head at Y; put the neck in place, hold in exact position and mark the top of it so it will fit the under side of the finger-board when the top of the latter is perfectly straight with the top of the box. Use a straight edge in doing this. Cut exactly to this line and square across and glue the finger-board in its exact position. Shape the neck and finger-board as indicated and round roughly as shown in sections at X. Fit them so the center lines of the finger-board and of the box will coincide and finish the under side of the head and neck as shown by dotted lines. Place glue blocks around the top of the rim of the box as at 4 so the top will rest upon them when it is glued in place.

Cut the 1 7/8- inch hole as shown, make the tail piece B of hard wood and glue it in place. The next day glue the neck and finger-board in place, being sure that the center lines are in true relation.

When the glue has thoroughly hardened sandpaper the body and finish the neck and finger-board with file and sandpaper. Bore the four ¼-inch peg holes as shown, using a round file or reamer to taper the hole so it will be somewhat larger on the bottom side. Make four pegs about 2 inches long with tapered shanks to fit these holes. A saw cut in the end of each peg will hold the string. Glue a small piece at V to finish the bottom of the neck.

Make the nut W of hard wood, cut the groove to receive it and glue it in place. Get out twelve frets C of tin or copper and bend them over as shown. This may be made of wider metal and cut to 3-32 inches width after bending. To locate the frets, string up the instruments and try with a piano or other instrument of fixed tone. Move a piece of wire back and forth until the correct pitch is attained. The octave fret of the open string should be about 6 ½ inches from the nut W, but this must be proved by trial. Find the octave first, then the 3rd, 5th and 7th, the 2nd, 4th and 6th and the half tones last. Make fine saw cuts 1/16 inch deep where the frets are to be placed and we are ready for finishing.

Stain if desired and give two coats of hard varnish. When thoroughly dry, clean out the cuts for the frets and set them in varnish, carefully removing any surplus. The string may be old violin strings or different sizes of wire though softer tones may be made with stout linen or silk thread.

1935 – Cigar Box Violin

In the February/March issues of *Popular Homecraft*, pp 338-339, plans for How to Make a Cigar Box Violin are published. This is not surprising. There are multiple sources in teaching guides that feature these easy to build instruments for young schoolchildren around 1935. However, it should be noted that these are plans for a full 4-string instrument. Similar plans or evidence of cigar box violins had fewer strings because they were easier to play. The bow often would not have clear access to the outer strings from the square box. For that reason, cigar box violins were often limited to three strings or less.

How to Make a Cigar Box Violin
By P. M. Pennell

Anyone who loves music and is handy with tools can easily make a cigar box violin that is capable of producing really good tones. The violin may be designed for either two strings or four, depending on the maker's ability as a craftsman and aspirations as a player.

The musical range of the four stringed instrument is the same as that of a real violin, but, although the two stringed instrument is easier to make and to play, it has the compass of nearly all well known songs and melodies. Under supervision, a group of children between the ages of 10 and 15 made some very creditable violins and later played them at several public affairs.

Materials include a wooden cigar box, a piece of broom or mop handle about 23" long, two smooth pieces of wood for fingerboard and tail piece, two small screw eyes, two (or four) ukulele pegs, a stout violin bridge, some short pieces of heavy wire, and glue, tiny nails and some extra pieces of wood for nut, sound post and bass bar. The two string violin requires violin A and D strings while the four stringed instrument uses a full set of violin strings. An old bow can be bought cheap at a music or second hand store.

As cigar boxes vary in shape and size, the measurements given here must necessarily be approximate, but by following the basic principles a playable violin will result. The children mentioned in an earlier paragraph built their instruments for four strings, but strung them up with only two until they had learned to play them. The children's fiddles had slightly shorter measurements.

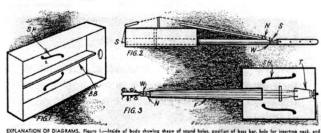

EXPLANATION OF DIAGRAMS. Figure 1.—Inside of body showing shape of sound holes, position of bass bar, hole for inserting neck, and a cross where end of sound post will be glued. Figure 2.—Side view of violin. Dotted lines on body show position of neck and sound post inside the violin. Figure 3.—Top of violin. Figure 4.—Diagram of tuning and positions for fingers on the strings.

BODY – Scrape paper label from the cigar box and sandpaper it. Make a paper patter the size of the bottom of the box and outline the sound holes, being careful not to have them too close together. Trace the outlines on the bottom of the box and cut out with a fine toothed jig saw. The bottom of the box will be the top of the violin.

BASS BAR – Cut a piece of wood, ¼" wide by ½" deep, and the length of the inside of the box. Spread the edge with glue and glue in place near the sound hole. (Study Fig. 1 for position). The bass bar braces the wood fibers of the top of the instrument on the side of the heavier strings.

NECK – Flatten the end of the broomstick on both sides for distance of about 5". In this flat part bore holes for the pegs about 1" apart. File the holes until the pegs, entering alternately from opposite sides, come through far enough for the string holes to be seen.

ATTACHING NECK TO BODY – Cut a hole large enough to admit broom handle in the end of the box. The edge of the hole should be about 1" from the top of the box with its sound holes, so that the fingerboard will slant at about the right

279

angle toward the bridge. Pass the neck through the hole to the other end outside with a screw eye and a few tiny nails (See Fig. 1 and 2.)

SOUND POST – Make a small round post as long as the depth of the box and a little less in thickness than a lead pencil. Glue the end in place as indicated by X in Fig 1. Now glue the cover on the bottom of the box and add a few nails around the edge to hold it tight.

The sound post conducts the sound vibrations to the back of the instrument (whence they emerge through the sound holes) and also supports the top.

NUT (also called little bridge) – Make a wedge shaped piece of wood 1" long and a little deeper than the thickness of the wood to be used for the fingerboard. Flatten a small space on top of the neck about 1 ½" from the pegs and on this glue the nut securely. The top of the nut should be slightly rounded and have two (or four) slight notches to space the strings and hold them just above the surface of the fingerboard. (Fig. 2 & 3, and photo of neck detail.)

FINGERBOARD – Cut a smooth piece of wood 10" long, 1" wide at one end and slightly wider at the other. (Fig. 3.) For the two stringed violin the top of the fingerboard may be left flat but for the four stringed violin it must be rounded to conform to the curve of the bridge and nut. Glue the fingerboard to the violin with its narrower end touching the nut and secure with a nail at the points where it touches the neck and body.

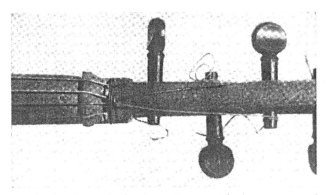

Detail of violin neck, showing strings stretched over nut, and under wire and screw eye to pegs.

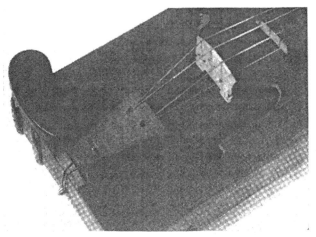

Top of violin, showing details of construction.

Between the nut and the pegs gouge out a place on the neck (Fig. 2 and photograph of neck). In this hollow put a screw eye to hold the A and D string in place. If four strings are to be used, bind a piece of wire around the neck and this point leaving an open space to pass the outer strings under. (See photo.)

TAIL PIECE – Cut a piece of wood 2 ¼" long. Shape as in Fig. 3. Drill two holes near each end. Fasten the smaller end to the screw eye in the end of the violin with a piece of strong wire. Just above the screw eye, on top of the violin at the edge, glue a small piece of wood about 1/8" thick. This keeps the wire from cutting into the body of the violin and keeps the tail piece from touching the top.

BRIDGE – File the feet of the bridge flat to fit the top of the violin. A high bridge is recommended. The top of the bridge should have two (or four) slight notches to space the strings evenly and keep them from slipping out of place. The strings in the holes in the tail piece pass over the bridge, fingerboard and nut. The two middle strings go through the screw eye and the two outer strings go under the wire to the pegs (Fig. 3, and photograph). As you hold the violin facing you, the strings reading from left to right are G, D, A, and E, tuned in fifths. For the two stringed violin only the D and A are used. The pressure of the strings holds the bridge in place but it will break unless kept standing up straight. The string length from bridge to nut should be about 12 to 13". If when playing on the G and E strings, the bow touches the edge of the instrument, the edges may be shaped off a bit with a rasp or coarse sandpaper.

A young maker tries out this cigar box violin.

1938 – How To Make A Japanese Fiddle

In 1938 Raymond S. Forbes throws the rules of the comma and other handy bits of punctuation to the wind in *The Boys' Make-And-Do Book* for his plans on how to build a one stringed Japanese fiddle. While Forbes goes into a lot of detail on how to build a wooden box, he does mention that one of these could be easily made from an ordinary cigar box.

Apart from the string, the cost is negligible if you make the whole of the instrument for yourself. Readers who have not got the tools, or the facilities, for much woodwork, will be able to buy the neck and the peg for about 1/6, and then all that they will have to do is to attach the sound box and fix the bridge pieces.

An ordinary cigar box can be used, but a box with a rounded end will be more satisfactory than a square one and will be quite easy to construct. If a piece of 1/8 in. plywood is used for the curved part.

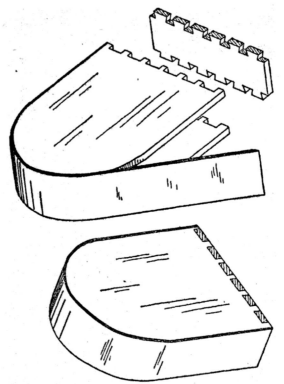

Fig. 1—Two views showing method of construction and the finished box.

The top and bottom of the box are 3/8 in. thick, and the plywood is glued and screwed around the edges, as shown in Fig. 1, using round headed screws.

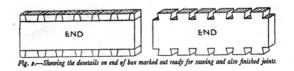

Fig. 2.—Showing the dovetails on end of box marked out ready for sawing and also finished joints.

The square end of the box is dovetailed in place, and in Fig. 2 is shown the method of marking out and, also, the finished joint. Make this end complete first, then place it in position and mark round the dovetails on to the ends of the top and bottom, then cut out the sockets into which the dovetails fit by sawing the sides and chiseling out the waste wood.

After the joints have all been fitted the end can be glued in place and, when the glue has set, cleaned up. Fig. 3 shows the top of the box drawn out on 1 in. squares to enable this part of the work to be marked down accurately without any trouble.

In order to transfer the vibrations from the top to the bottom of the box, a sound post must be fitted, vertically, from the middle of the space in between the holes down to the bottom. A piece of 1/4 inch diameter dowel rod can be used for this, and should be cut so that it is a tight fit and will remain in place. If the plywood is screwed on one side and over the rounded end, the sound post can be inserted and then the remainder of the plywood screwed in position.

This part of the fiddle should, preferably, be made out of a piece of hardwood such as walnut, mahogany or birch. All the important dimensions are shown in Fig. 4.

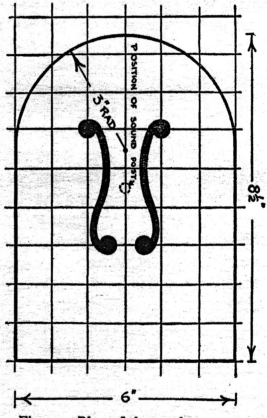

Fig. 3.—Plan of the top drawn out on
1 in. squares—this will enable it to be
marked out quite easily.

The neck is notched out at the end so that it fits round the square and of the box; the part marked A should be grouped into the box to a depth of 1/8 in. to prevent any sideways movement, and the part B glued and screwed on to the bottom of the box.

288

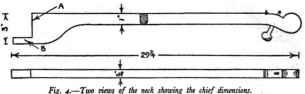

Fig. 4.—Two views of the neck showing the chief dimensions.

The peg, also, must be made of a straight grained piece of hardwood and the dimensions for this are shown in Fig. 5. Unless you particularly wish to make the whole instrument yourself, it is hardly worth the while making the peg, as there is a good deal of work in it and a suitable one can be bought for twopence.

Fig. 6 shows the position of the peg in the neck. A hole, 1/4 in. in diameter should be bored at the angle shown, and then the necessary taper filled out, with a small "rat-tail" file. Care must be taken to ensure the peg eating a good fit, otherwise it is liable to work loose and turn round, thus altering the tension on the string.

On the far end of the box, a round-headed screw should be inserted in the middle of the thickness of the top. To this one in of the string is attached.

The next job is to make and fit the two bridge pieces that raise the string above the sound box and the neck. These must be made out of a piece of hardwood and, if let into the wood to a depth of 1/8 in. and carefully glued, will not need any further fixing. The one on the box should be fitted directly over the sound post.

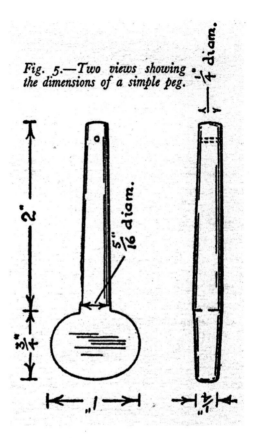

Fig. 5.—Two views showing the dimensions of a simple peg.

The whole of the work can now receive its final glasspapering, and will then be ready for polishing. If you have had previous experience of polishing, this will be quite straightforward, but novices at the art can also carry out this part of the work quite satisfactorily.

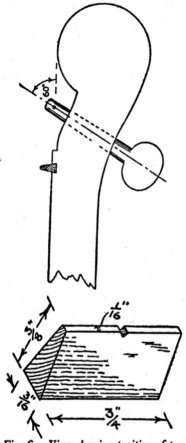

*Fig. 6.—View showing position of peg
and rear bridge, and dimensioned view
of one of the bridges.*

A coating of wax polish must first be rubbed into
the wood, with a clean rag, to fill up the pores,
and then two or three coats of French polish
applied to it with a 1 in. flat camel-hair brush until
the required finish has been obtained. To get the
best finish put the polish on very thinly and work

in the direction in which the grain of the wood goes; also, always allow one coat to dry thoroughly before the next is applied.

Finally, fit the string to the screw at one end and thread the other end through the hole in the peg.

1939 – It's Fun to Make a One-String Fiddle Like Irby's

Included in the rear of Erick Berry's *One-String Fiddle* were these all too easy to remove plans to make a one-string fiddle from a cigar box.

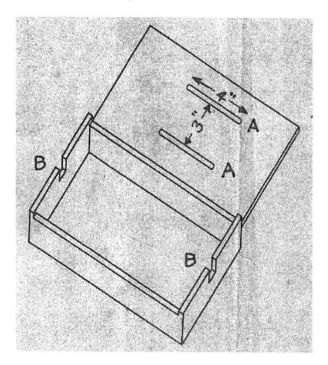

MATERIALS you need:

1. Cigar box.
2. Soft wood stick, 1" square and 24" long.
3. Piece of soft wood, ¼" thick, 1" wide, 3" long.
4. Piece of soft wood, ¼" thick, 1" wide, 2" long.
5. Glue

TOOLS you will need:

A sharp knife.
A ¼" drill or auger.
A small piece of coarse sandpaper.

1. Cutting the Cigar Box

First cut the tone openings in the lid A and A. Here's the easiest way: Drill two rows of ¼" holes and then cut the rest of the wood away to make straight slits 4" long. The slits should be 3" apart.

Cut Square Holes for stick at B and B in the ends of the box. Make them just the size of your stick, and just deep enough for lid to close.

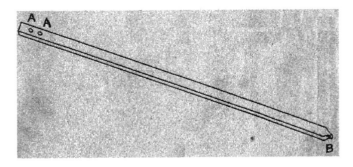

2. Cutting the Stick

Drill two ¼" holes, A and A, through the stick about an inch apart. Be sure that the end hole is an inch in from the tip of the stick and is nice and smooth.

Sharpen the other end of the stick to a blunt point, B.

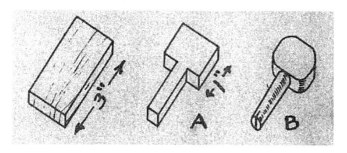

3. Making the Peg

Take the piece of soft wood 3" long and cut it out to shape A. Be sure the bottom part is ¼" wide. Round off the corners of the top part and with your knife carefully whittle the bottom part round. Finish this bottom part or stem by twisting it within a roll of sandpaper until it fits tightly in the end hole of the stick. Cut a notch in the end of the stem.

4. Making the Bridge

Cut one side of the 2" piece of soft wood to make a sharp edge and put a light notch in the center of it.

ASSEMBLING

Put glue on the edges of the square holes in the box and force the stick all the way down in them with the pointed end jutting out slightly. Then put glue on the stick where the closed lid touches and around edges of lid. Close the lid and put a weight on it to hold it down until the glue dries.

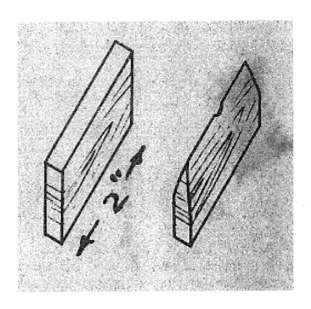

FINISHING

After the stick and box are glued, glue the bridge on the box between the tone openings.

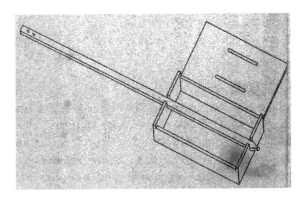

Put the peg in the outside hole. Tie a loop in one end of the violin string. Slip this over the pointed end of the stick. Run the string over the notch in the bridge, then through the second hole in the stick and wrap it around the peg three or four times. Slip the end of the string in the notch of the peg. Turn the peg to tighten the string.

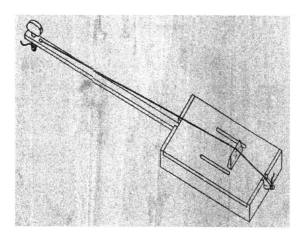

TUNING THE FIDDLE

With your left hand, turn the peg while you pluck the string with the thumb of your right. Tune it to the tone pitch most pleasing to your ear.

1948 – One String Cigar Box Violin

Cigar Box Violin by W.J. Sutherland publishes in the February/March issue of *Science and Mechanics*, his historic plans on how to build a 1-string cigar box violin.

After you've smoked the cigars, you can make music with the box they came in. It's an easy job to make a cigar box violin, so let's begin. First remove lid from cigar box (B in Fig. 4). Cut out hole 2 ¼ inches in diameter with a fret saw or pen knife. Then cut a piece of broom handle, quarter it and cut in lengths the same as depth of cigar box (A in Fig. 4). Next glue quartered pieces in four corners of cigar box. This will reinforce the box and also improve the tone. Sandpaper inside of cigar box and apply two coats of shellac, allowing first coat to dry before putting on the second.

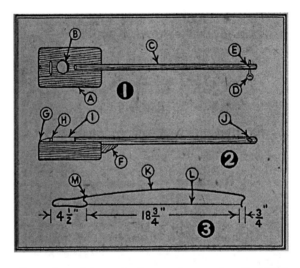

Finger board is made from a broom handle 27 ½ inches long and 1 inch in diameter (C in Fig. 4). On one end cut out a piece 2 ½ inches long halfway through handle. Then glue finger board (broom handle) to lid (B in Fig. 4) and secure with small woodscrew. Drill screw hole to prevent splitting. Put screw in from up through lid into handle. At other end of finger board (E in Fig. 4) drill 3/8 inch hole 1 inch from end through from top to bottom. This is so string can wind on D (Fig. 4). Then make saw cut at edge of hole to set in piece of brass 1/16 inch thick, ¾ inch wide and 3/16 inch high. A small notch is cut in brass with edge of file to keep string centered (J in Fig. 4). The piece of brass prevents string from cutting into handle or finger board. Another hole, ¼ inch, is drilled at right angles through 3/8 inch hole already drilled. This hole is for peg (D in Fig. 4). Peg is tapered, therefore ¼ inch hole must also be tapered. This is easily done by wrapping a piece of fine sandpaper once around peg. With a rotating motion sand ¼ inch hole to taper of peg. Take sandpaper off peg and fit frequently. This is important. When string is strained peg is pushed into tapered hole and must hold at desired position when tuned. A supporting bracket is made from a piece of wood 2 ½ inches long, 1 ½ inches wide, and ½ inch thick (F in Fig. 4) and glued to box and finger board and secured with two small nails.

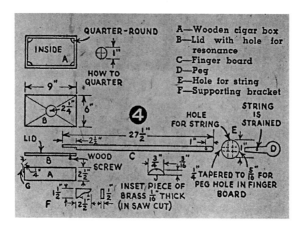

You are now ready to sandpaper box and finger board. Apply two coats of shellac allowing first coat to dry. Use fine sandpaper again before second coat is applied. Tail piece is made of brass 1 ½ inches long, ½ inch wide and 1/16 inch thick (G in Fig. 5). Drill hole 1/16 inch in diameter centered 1/8 inch from end. Then slot with hacksaw. Slightly bend ¼ inch from top; this prevents string from slipping out. (String should have a piece of metal secured on end as anchor.) From other end of tail piece drill 1/8 inch hole ¼ inch from end, and another 1/8 inch hole ¾ inch higher. These holes are centered. Tail piece is fastened to end of box, ¼ inch above surface of box (G and A in Fig. 4). Bend in tail piece should project from box.

H in Fig. 5 should be the bridge, made from a piece of hardwood 3/16 inch at the bottom tapered to 1/8 inch at top, 1 ¾ inches wide, and approximately 5/8 inch high. Bridge should hold string 1/8 inch off finger board. Bridge should be half way between resonance hole and tail piece. Bridge will remain in position when string is tightened or strained.

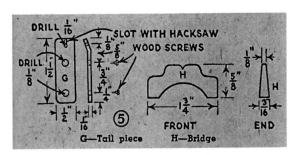

Bow can be made from wire coat hanger (K in Fig. 3). First straighten and form as shown in diagram. End of wire is soldered to form handle on bow as shown in M in Fig. 3. Then a spool of fine white silk thread is tied at one end of bow and stranded to other end of bow (L in Fig. 3). Thread tight enough to keep thread taut. When ready to use rub thread over a piece of rosin. If you have a regular violin bow, you can, of course, use it instead of making one. Peg shown (D in Fig. 1) is a regular violin peg. You'll find that a guitar 3rd string, if you have one, gives best results. And peg, rosin and string can be purchased at a music store in your neighborhood.

The cigar box violin is played by holding box between the knees with finger board resting on the left shoulder; this allows free use of hands. The bow is held in right hand and drawn over string; left hand index-finger is placed on string. Finger is moved up and down pressing string against finger board to get the desired notes. The violin has a range of two and a half octaves, and should be tuned to G on piano.

1951 – Boing Box

Two similar projects from Robert B. Turnbull's *Radio and Television Sound Effects* don't specify cigar boxes as part of their construction. However, the appearance and construction of the Boing Box is a monochord instrument that could be played like any other. Or, perhaps the reverse is true and one string fiddles should be played by bending their necks.

Boing Box

The device is similar in sound to the TWANG BOX, but its construction and operation are different. The boing box gives the comedy sound "Boooooiiiiiinnnnnnnnngggggggg!"

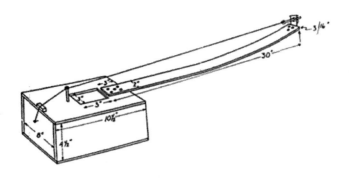

The chief components of the boing box are the resonating body, steel wire, and flexible neck.

Construct the box to the dimensions given using well-seasoned 1/2-in. (12.7 mm) wood, except the face which should be made of 1/4-in. (6.35 mm) three-ply. The box should be accurately cut and fitted, and fastened together with countersunk flat-head screws.

Cut a 3-in. (76 mm) square hole in the top surface of the box. The upright screw eye (bridge) should be about 2 1/2 or 3 in. (63-76 mm) long and solidly screwed into the top about an inch from the sounding hole. The 30-in. (762 mm) flexible neck should be made of 3/16 in. (4.76 mm) plywood, 2 in. (50 mm) wide, or of the same dimension flexible metal. Securely bolt one end of the neck to the sounding box.

At the other end of the neck bolt a 2-in. (50 mm) right-angle bracket. Pass an eye bolt through the projecting part of the angle iron, and secure at the outside with a lock washer and wing nut.

The wire should be 10-gauge .024-in. (.6 mm) diameter tinned music wire. The Johnson Steel and Wire Company manufactures a satisfactory wire in 25-ft. lengths that sells for thirty cents which may be obtained in most hardware stores. Attach the wire to the screw eye on the side of the box, run up over the top edge of the box, through the upright screw eye, and fasten to the eye bolt. Tighten the wing nut until the tension on the wire definitely bows the neck of the instrument.

To get the "boing", pluck the tautened wire and shake the box vigorously so the neck vibrates. A little practice will show how tight to draw the wire and how rapidly to vibrate the box.

Twang Box

This is the device that makes the comedy sound, "Twaaaannngggg."

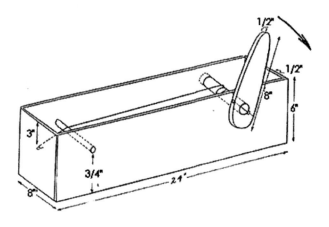

Build a wooden box to the dimensions given. At one end insert a 1/2 to 3/4 -inch (12-19 mm) piece of pipe and anchor it firmly to the sides of the box. At the other end use a piece of 1-in. (25 mm) wooden dowel rod. Fasten a wooden handle to the rod as shown in the drawing. This rod must be able to rotate freely. At the end of the box the farthest distance from the rod and handle, attach a piece of 10-guage 0.024-in. (.06 mm) diameter tinned music wire so that it is anchored slightly below the metal rod that runs across the box. Run the wire to the 1-in. rod (with handle) and wrap it a couple of turns around the rod, then fasten that end of the wire securely to the dowel rod.

To use, pull the handle in the direction of the heavy arrow just enough to take up the slack in the wire. With the free hand pluck the wire, then instantly jerk the handle back and forth so as to alternately release and tighten the tension on the wire.

A little practice will show just how much tension on the wire and how much pull on the handle will give the desired effect. The boing box gives a similar effect except that usually the tone of the sound is higher and the instrument can be worked faster.

The top of the twang box is open, there being no cover on it.

1951 – Rubber Band Cigar Box Guitar

Relegated to children's play things, the cigar box guitar degenerates to a set of rubber bands around an old box. From *The Post-Standard*, October 6, 1951:

Homemade Guitar Proves Easy to Make

Most children love to play with sound. At first it's the sound they can make with their lips. Then, there's the banging and clanging that comes from pots and pans, pieces of wood, or what have you. A little later, they will enjoy recorded music. And, of course they'll sing themselves.

Now and again, it's fun to have an instrument of your own even tho [sic] you're only three, four or five years of age. A drum is noisy but good. Water glasses filled to different heights give out some interesting sounds.

But here's something a little more unusual and very simple to make. It's a cigar-box guitar. All you do is take a wooden cigar box, or any similar sized box, remove the top and stretch rubber bands of different widths lengthwise over the box. When these "strings" are plucked, they will make different sounds and tho [sic] it is not easy to play a real tune, there's a lot of fun in just playing.

1954 – Rubber Band Cigar Box Guitar

In the *Oakland Tribune*, May 9, 1954, the rubber band cigar box guitar appears again:

I hope that you have had the fun of being a part of a rhythm band at some time. These bands are fun for all, for homemade instruments are used. You can blow into bottles, use pie plates with bottle caps, pan lids to bang together, and how about cigar box guitar? You will need a cigar box, some rubber bands, and a small piece of wood for a bridge. This is not the kind of bridge that people use to walk over, but a bridge that strings go over for tone.

The bridge can be made from soft wood, and you can make it go about half way across the cigar box. Whittle it so that the top is more narrow than the bottom. Finish it with sand paper to give it a finished look, then make four notches in the top.

Use a jig saw to cut a half oval in the lid of the box. This should go about half way across too, and should be about an inch and a half wide at the widest part. Set the bridge about two inches down from this. Use rubber bands of regular length, and put these around the box the long way. Set the bridge in place and have the rubber bands run through the notches. This makes a good strumming instrument. Sing and play for fun.

1975 – Rubber Band Cigar Box Banjo

In *Prof. Hammerfingers' Indestructible Toys*, Steve Ross, October 1975, Oliver Press, p 203 Ross presents plans for another rubber band banjo with a non-functional spoon-like wooden piece for a "neck."

CIGAR BOX BANJO [which, by the way does not use a cigar box at all!]

Materials needed:
  1 pc. 53" x 3/4" x 3-1/2" (milled 1"x4") for box and handle

Upholstery tacks
Rubber bands
5d nails

This is one of the quieter musical toys. After personal experience with drums, triangle, horns and assorted cacophonies I decided to include this banjo for my nerves and yours.

Cut one 24" piece, two 8" pieces, and one 5" piece (2-1/2") and measure 1-3/4" each way from the center and mark. Measure 3/4" in from the edge at these marks and mark again. Draw a line between these marks. Say 3/4" into this line at each end. Using a chisel, cut out the 3/4" x 3-1/2" rectangle. Repeat with the other 5" piece. Sand all pieces.

Nail the box together as shown. Fit the handle in the slots and nail it to the box. Nail the upholstery tack along the top and bottom of the box as shown. String rubber bands of different thicknesses between the tacks and play. If for some unknown reason you want to make the banjo louder, nail a piece of 1/4" plywood over the back.

1976 – Cigar Box Guitar

December 1976, *Guitar Player* magazine featured Michael Lydon's article A Great American Tradition, The Cigar Box Guitar, which begins with a quote from Carl Perkins.

Before I went to school, I started fooling around on a guitar. My daddy made me one with a cigar box, a broomstick, and two strands of bailing wire and I'd sit and beat on that thing.

\- Carl Perkins

Like Carl Perkins' daddy, I've made a 2-string cigar box guitar, and like Carl Perkins, I've been beating on it. It sounds good, particularly played bottleneck and tuned to an open chord. It gives strong volume with a clear ring to it, and it can deliver smooth Hawaiian swoops and bluesy clangs. The cost: less than a dollar; the tools: a saw, coping saw, hand drill, pocket knife and chisel, white glue, and sandpaper. It took thought but no hard work, and I think I've learned something about the guitar I didn't know before. Plus I have a brand new axe I'm proud of.

I made it because I wanted to study from scratch what happens when a taut string vibrates. Nailing one end of a guitar string to a board, tugging the other, and twanging the middle wasn't good enough. My arm got tired, and the string made a sound, but not a loud one. The solution was to fasten both ends of the string and to get the string's vibration to in turn vibrate something else larger and more resonant. So for 84¢ I bought 3' of wood 1 ½" square (a 2x2 in lumberyard parlance) and got a cigar box free from a liquor store.

My first idea: run the 2x2 *through* the cigar box so that the strings, attached at both ends to the same piece of wood, would span out but put no pressure on the cardboard box. I cut holes in either end of the cigar box about 3/8" from the top, then whittled off about 3/8" off the top of the 2x2 along enough length for the whittled part to go through the box. The "fingerboard" section was level with the top of the cigar box, and what was inside was recessed enough so the box top, soon to be the soundboard, didn't touch it. At the tailpiece piece end I replaced what I had pared away so it too was at the fingerboard level.

Bridge to nut on my Gibson acoustic guitar is about two feet; that seemed fine for this one. I cut the 2x2 accordingly, angling the cut to make a slanted plate for the tuning pegs, again imitating the Gibson. Whittling the insert cutaway for the gears took some figuring, and I did a trial run on the extra part of the 2x2 I had cut off. To hold the string at the tailpiece I drilled two holes to run the strings through from the back, adding two buttons in back to keep the string ends from being tugged into the wood – my first fancy touch.

Nut and bridge on the Gibson are bone, so I sawed little piece from a beef soup bone and sanded them to shape.

For the all important soundboard I first used some corrugated paper sent to me around a record. The first time I tightened the strings, it began to cave in. I added a plywood strip crosswise as bracing, notching the 2x2 so it would clear. After a few days of playing, it began to warp again. Only then did I think: why not use the nice stiff original top of the cigar box? This I braced crosswise and also diagonally on either side of the sound hole. It's both sturdy and tensile and works fine.

No truss rod adjustment needed with a neck like this.

Finishing touches: a piece of abalone shell cut in the neck and an L monogram in silver paint that curls around the tuning pegs. I oiled the wood with five coats of a mixture of linseed oil and turpentine, sanding the wood and rubbing it down between coats. It feels satiny and has a nice golden glow. I string it with the third and fourth strings from my Gibson when I change strings on that.

When I was making the cigar box guitar I pretty nearly crushed it twice out of plain carelessness, and a few times, when I couldn't figure out my next step, I felt like smashing it in frustration. I'm glad I got it done in one piece. It tickles me to own a unique guitar – the one and only Lydon – and the thrill I get playing it is priceless.

1998 – Rubber Band Cigar Box Guitar

365 More Simple Science Experiments With Everyday Objects
[Black Dog & Leventhal Publishers, Inc., 1998, page 60]
published "plans" for a cigar box guitar made from
rubber bands on an empty box. While I disagree with
calling such a creation a guitar, the number of times this
noise maker is suggested in the timeline deserves
mentioning.

Years ago, people made their own musical
instruments. They loved music, but instruments
were expensive and they had little money to buy
them. Today, right now, you can do the same
thing.

What to do: Open the lid of the cigar box and keep it open (or remove it altogether). Now, beginning with the widest rubber band, then to the next-to-the-widest, place them lengthwise around the cigar box. Try to space the rubber bands equally, about one finger-width apart. When you have all six "guitar strings" in place, give each of them a pluck.

What happens: The wide rubber band has a low sound, the very narrow "string" has a high sound, and the sounds of the other rubber bands are somewhere in between.

Why: The wide rubber band has a low vibration rate and does not produce many sound waves. The narrow rubber band, however, has a high vibration rate and produces a higher number of sound waves with a higher tone or pitch. But that's not all. Pitch also depends on the degree of tightness, or tautness, of the "string." A wider but short rubber band that is pulled very tight might make a higher sound than a narrower rubber band that is put on more loosely.

What next: Listen to the sounds of each of your instrument's strings again. If needed, switch them around so that the sounds are in order, from lowest to highest. When you are ready, sing a tune and accompany yourself on your cigar box guitar.

Works Cited

1. "The Aeolian Harp." *The Geneva Express* 3 May 1856: 1. Print.

2. "Allen 'Farina' Hoskins (1920 - 1980) - Find A Grave Memorial." *Find A Grave - Millions of Cemetery Records.* N.p., n.d. Web. 21 Sept. 2009. <http://www.findagrave.com/cgi-bin/fg.cgi?page=gr&GRid=8483>.

3. *American Life Histories: Manuscripts from the Federal Writers' Project*, 1936-1940, no W9647. 10 Oct. 1940. Submission by Sara B. Wrenn, March 17, 1939, <u>Oregon Folklore Studies</u>, informant Frank E. Coulter.

4. Ancelet, Barry J., Jay Edwards, and Glen Pitre. *Cajun Country.* Jackson: Mississippi UP, 1991. Print.

5. Anderson, Chuck. "Home's Where Piano Is, and It's Grand." *Oakland Tribune* 17 Oct. 1976, sec. H: 2. Print.

6. Ashby, Leroy. *With Amusement for All A History of American Popular Culture Since 1830.* New York: Kentucky UP, 2006. Print.

7. Aswell, James. "My New York." *The Oshkosh Northwestern* 8 Sept. 1937: 15. Print.

8. Barnum, Phineas Taylor. *Struggles and triumphs, or Forty years' recollections of P.T. Barnum.* Buffalo: Courier Company, 1875. Print.

9. Barnum, Phineas Taylor. *The autobiography of P.T. Barnum: clerk, merchant, editor, and showman.* London: Ward and Lock, 1855. Print.

10. Bass Bargaingram. Advertisement. *Scientific American* Apr. 1938: 243. Print.

11. Beard, Daniel C. *Hardly a Man Is Now Alive: The Autobiography of Dan Beard.* New York: Doubleday, 1939. Print.

12. Beard, Daniel Carter. "Christmas Eve With Uncle Enos." *The Book Buyer* 1.10 (1884): 311-14. Print.

13. Beloff, Jim. *The Ukulele A Visual History.* New York: Backbeat Books, 2003. Print.

14. Benedetto, Robert. *Making an Archtop Guitar.* Anaheim Hills (California): Centerstream, 1994. Print.

15. "Benefit Dance For Army Band." *Fitchburg Daily Sentinel* 24 Apr. 1918: n. pag. Print.

16. Bernard, Shane K. *Swamp Pop: Cajun and Creole Rhythm and Blues.* Jackson: Mississippi UP, 1996. Print.

17. Berry, Erick. *One-String Fiddle.* Eau Claire: E. M. Hale And Company, 1939. Print.

18. "Bizarre sound effects." *Bizarre Stuff You Can Make in Your Kitchen.* Web. 08 Feb. 2010. <http://bizarrelabs.com/boing2.htm>.

19. Bolin, Frances Schoonmaker, ed. *Poetry for Young People Carl Sandburg (Poetry For Young People)*. New York: Sterling, 2008. Print.

20. *The Boy Mechanic, Book 3, 800 Things for Boys to Do*. Chicago: Popular Mechanics, 1919. Print.

21. Boyle, Hal. "Things We Can All Do Without." *Fitchburg (Mass.) Sentinel* 24 Jan. 1964: 6. Print.

22. Breckenridge, Judy, Anthony D. Fredericks, and Louis V. Loeschnig. *365 More Simple Science Experiments with Everyday Materials*. New York: Black Dog & Leventhal, 1998. Print.

23. Browne, Lewis Allen. "Adventure Trails Blazed For You." *Aunt Elsie Magazine Of The Oakland Tribune* 8 Oct. 1922: n. pag. Print.

24. Browne, Lewis Allen. "Adventure Trails Blazed For You." *The Janesville Daily Gazette* 25 Jan. 1923: n. pag. Print.

25. Burman, Ben L. *Blow for a Landing*. New York: Mockingbird Books, 1974. Print.

26. Cantwell, Robert. *Bluegrass Breakdown: The Making of the Old Southern Sound (Music in American Life)*. New York: Illinois UP, 2002. Print.

27. Carlin, Bob. *String Bands in the North Carolina Piedmont*. Boston: McFarland & Company, 2004. Print.

28. "Catholic News." *The Sunday Light* 1 Mar. 1896: 1. Print.

29. "Church Members Hold Picnic." *The Logansport Morning Press* 21 July 1921: n. pag. Print.

30. "Cigar Box Fiddler Becomes Overseas Star." *Middletown Daily Times-Express* 2 Sept. 1919: n. pag. Print.

31. "Cigar Box Fiddles Are Easy To Make." *The Sandusky Star Journal* 24 June 1921: n. pag. Print.

32. "Cigar Box Guitars." *Cigar Box Guitars - Join the Revolution.* Web. 05 Oct. 2009. <http://cigarboxguitars.com/museum/History.php>.

33. Coleman, Satis N. *Creative Music for Children.* New York: Kinckerbocker: G. P. Putnam's Sons, 1922. Print.

34. Cord, W. F. "Musical Instruments from Cigar Boxes." *Popular Mechanics* Sept. 1923: 485-86. Print.

35. Dean, Arthur. "Your Boy and Your Girl." *The Olean Evening Times* 11 Mar. 1929: n. pag. Print.

36. Dean, Arthur. "Your Boy and Your Girl." *The Olean Evening Times* 8 Mar. 1929: n. pag. Print.

37. DeSalvo, Debra. *The Language of the Blues From Alcorub to Zuzu.* New York: Billboard Books, 2006. Print.

38. "Doc Watson." *PBS ? Austin City Limits.* N.p., n.d. Web. <http://www.pbs.org/klru/austin/artists/program274.html>

39. Doucet, Sharon Arms. *Fiddle Fever.* New York: Clarion Books, 2000. Print.

40. Doucet, Sharon Arms. "'If You Remember My Song, You'll Remember Me' An Interview with Canray Fontenot." *Fiddler Magazine* Fall 1995: n. pag. Print.

41. Edgar, Walter B. "Jenkins Orphanage." *The South Carolina Encyclopedia.* Columbia, SC: University of South Carolina, 2006. 590-91. Print.

42. Ewen, David. *Popular American Composers from Revolutionary Times to the Present.* New York: H. W. Wilson Company, 1962. Print.

43. "Exhibit Traces Changes In the American Guitar." *The Daily Herold* [Tyrone, PA] 7 June 1994: 6. Print.

44. Ferris, William. *Blues from the Delta.* New York: Da Capo, 1988. Print.

45. Ferris, William, ed. *Afro-American folk art and crafts.* Jackson: Mississippi UP, 1983. Print.

46. "Fields in 'Poppy,' Lederer In Paris Farce at Alameda." *Oakland Tribune* 8 Aug. 1936: n. pag. Print.

47. "FolkStreams Dry Wood Bois Sec and Canray." *Folkstreams The Best of American Folklore Films.* N.p., n.d. Web. 21 Sept. 2009. <http://www.folkstreams.net/context,42>.

48. "For Rapid Reading." *The Bucks County Gazette* [Bristol, PA] 3 Apr. 1908: 1. Print.

49. Forbes, Edwin. *A Civil War Artist at the Front: Edwin Forbes' Life Studies of the Great Army.* Ed. William F. Dawson. New York: Oxford UP, 1957. Print.

50. Forbes, Edwin. *Thirty years after an artist's memoir of the Civil War*. Baton Rouge: Louisiana State UP, 1993. Print.

51. Forbes, Raymond S. *The Boys' Make-and-Do Book*. London: Collins, 1938. Print.

52. "From Revolution to Reconstruction: Outlines: Outline of American Literature: The Rise of Realism: 1860-1914: Vachel Lindsay (1879-1931)." N.p., n.d. Web. 21 Sept. 2009. <http://www.let.rug.nl/usa/LIT/lindsay.htm>.

53. Gabbis, Howard R. "Uncle Wiggily and Sammie's Banjo." *The Ogden Standard Examiner* 14 Aug. 1920: n. pag. Print.

54. "GI Bookshelf." *The Stars and Stripes Magazine* 1 Sept. 1945: Vii. Print.

55. *Good For What Ails You: Music of the Medicine Shows 1926-1937*. Liner Notes. Old Hat Records / Enterprises. October 4, 2005. Print.

56. Graham, Joe Stanley. *Hecho En Tejas Texas-Mexican Folk Arts and Crafts (Publications of the Texas Folklore Society)*. New York: North Texas UP, 1997. Print.

57. Hal Leonard Corp. *All Music Guide to Country The Definitive Guide to Country Music*. New York: Backbeat Books, 2003. Print.

58. Hall, Albert Neely. *Handicraft for Handy Boys*. Boston: Lothrop, Lee & Shepard Co., 1911. Print.

59. Hasluck, Paul. *Violins and Other Stringed Instruments and How to Make Them*. Bradley IL: Lindsay Publications Inc, 1999. Print.

60. Heron-Allen, Edward. *Violin-Making A Historical and Practical Guide*. Minneapolis: Dover Publications, 2005. Print.

61. Hill, Edwin C. "Rivers and Dictators." *San Antonio Light* 29 Apr. 1938: n. pag. Print.

62. Hine, Thomas. *The Total Package The Secret History and Hidden Meanings of Boxes, Bottles, Cans, and Other Persuasive Containers*. New York: Back Bay Books, 1997. Print.

63. "A Home-made Banjo." *The Agitator* [Wellsboro, PA] 7 Sept. 1886: n. pag. Print. Duplicate of concise Uncle Enos Banjo plans.

64. "A Home-made Banjo." *The Oshkosh Daily Northwestern* 9 Mar. 1885, Evening ed.: n. pag. Print. Both a review of D. C. Beard's book, and concise directions to build an Uncle Enos Banjo.

65. "Homemade Guitar Proves Easy to Make." *The Post-Standard* 6 Oct. 1951: 16. Print.

66. Horvath, Betty. *Jasper Makes Music*. New York: Franklin Watts, Inc., 1967. Print.

67. "Hot Wells Open Air Cafe." *San Antonio Light And Gazette* 7 Aug. 1910: 8. Print.

68. "Hot Wire Guitar." *Practical Electrics* June 1924: 453. Print.

69. "How to make a cheap violin." *The Penny Magazine* 30 July 1838: 246-47. Print.

70. "How to Make Door Zither From Cigar Box." *The Syracuse Herald* 28 Feb. 1912, Evening ed.: 13. Print.

71. Hyman, Tony. *Handbook of Cigar Boxes.* Elmira, New York: Arnot Art Museum, 1979. Print.

72. Hyman, Tony. "Made_from_boxes." *National Cigar Museum.* N.p., n.d. Web. 21 Sept. 2009. <http://www.nationalcigarmuseum.com/Spe cial_Exhibits/Made_from_boxes.html>.

73. "In The Theatres." *The Olean Evening Herald* 28 Sept. 1920: n. pag. Print.

74. "An Ingenious Performer." *Chester Times* 18 Apr. 1918: n. pag. Print.

75. Irwin, John Rice. *Musical instruments of the Southern Appalachian Mountains.* 2nd ed. West Chester, Pa: Schiffer Ltd., 1983. Print.

76. Jacobs, A. J. *The Know-It-All.* New York: Simon & Schuster Paperbacks, 2004. Print.

77. "John King Says." Message to the author. 14 Dec. 2007. E-mail. Dispute evidence of Nunes cigar box ukulele.

78. Johnson, Grace. "Primitive Music for Little Primitives." *Good Housekeeping* June 1920: n. pag. Print.

79. "Joseph Hine's genuine "Amatic" Violin." *Iowa State Reporter* [Waterloo] 20 Aug. 1885: n. pag. Print.

80. Ketchum, Jr., William C. *Boxes.* Ed. Nancy Akre. Washington D. C.: Cooper-Hewitt Museum: Smithsonian Institution, 1982. Print.

81. Keynton, Tom. *Homemade musical instruments.* New York: Drake, 1975. Print.

82. King, Charles Albert. "The Handy Boy At Home." *Comfort Magazine* Oct. 1931: n. pag. Print.

83. King, Charles Albert. "The Handy Boy at Home." *The Charleston Daily Mail* 24 Mar. 1922, Evening ed.: n. pag. Print.

84. "Kitchen Utensils Lend a Hand in Odd Music of Cowboy Band." *Popular Science* Nov. 1940: 105. Print.

85. Kuprin, Alexandre. *Gambrinus and other Stories.* Trans. Bernard G. Guerney. New York: Adelphi Company, 1925. Print.

86. Leary, James P. *In tune with tradition Wisconsin folk musical instruments.* Wisconsin: Cedarburg Cultural Center, 1990. Print.

87. Lewin, Jim. *Witness to the Civil War First-Hand Accounts from Frank Leslie's Illustrated Newspaper.* New York: Collins, 2006. Print.

88. Lindsay, Vachel. *Going to the Stars.* New York: D. Appleton and Company, 1926. Print.

89. Linn, Karen. *That Half-Barbaric Twang: The Banjo in American Popular Culture.* Urbana: Illinois UP, 1994. Print.

90. Loder, Kurt. "A classic blues life." *Rolling Stone* 18 Mar. 1982: 17-18. Print.

91. Lomax, Alan. *The Land Where Blues Began.* Bloomington: Delta, 1994. Print.

92. Lydon, Michael. "A Great American Tradition, The Cigar Box Guitar." *Guitar Player* Dec. 1976: 80-82. Print.

93. M, H. J. "Two American Poets." *Independent* 117 (18 Sept. 1926): 331. Print.

94. "Mance Lipscomb Biography : OLDIES.com." *OLDIES.com : Direct Source for Collectables Records & Alpha Video - Oldies, Doo Wop, Jazz, Pop, Rock Music and Horror, Serials, Thrillers, Sci-Fi, Westerns Movies.* Web. 03 Oct. 2009. <http://www.oldies.com/artist-biography/Mance-Lipscomb.html>.

95. "Many Meetings Today." *Chester Times* 20 May 1918: n. pag. Print.

96. Martin, J. T. W. "REJUVENATING MUSICAL INSTRUMENTS." *The Times* 3 Mar. 1927: 2. Print.

97. "Matches, Pieces Of Hickory, Door Panel And Cigar Box Used By Port Arthur Youth In Making Fiddle That Plays." *The Port Arthur News* 26 Oct. 1935: 8. Print.

98. "Maya Angelou - Biography." *Maya Angelou - The Official Website.* Web. 04 Oct. 2009. <http://mayaangelou.com/bio/>.

99. Maya., Angelou,. *I Know Why the Caged Bird Sings.* New York: Virago Books, 1993. Print.

100. McIntyre, O. O. "Day by Day." *Logansport Pharos-Tribune* 31 Jan. 1936: 5. Print.

101. McIntyre, O. O. "Day by Day." *Olean Times-Herald* 31 Jan. 1936: 16. Print.

102. McIntyre, O. O. "New York Day by Day." *Logansport Pharos-Tribune* 13 Oct. 1922: 4. Print.

103. McMinnes, R.N., W. G. *Practical Flying: Complete Course of Flying Instruction.* New York: George H. Doran Company, 1918. Print.

104. Menn, Donn, ed. *Secrets From the Masters: Conversations With Forty Great Guitar Players From the Pages of Guitar Player Magazine.* San Fransico: Miller Freeman Books, 1992. Print.

105. "Mop Plays Tune, Boxes Hum In Real "Tin Pan Alley" Band." *The Galveston Daily News* 8 May 1932: 15. Print.

106. Mott, Robert L. *Radio Sound Effects Who Did It, and How, in the Era of Live Broadcasting.* Boston: McFarland & Company, 2005. Print.

107. Mottola, R. M. "A Method for Generating Rapid Prototypes of the Flattop Guitar." *American Lutherie: The Quarterly Journal of the Guild of American Luthiers* Winter 2006: 42-47. Print.

108. "Music 'Fan' Makes 'Cello Of Old Box." *Parade Of Youth* 1 May 1938: 3. Print.

109. "A Negro's Fiddle." *The Galveston Daily News* 17 May 1887: n. pag. Print.

110. "Ohio O. A. B. C. convention." *Lancaster Daily Eagle* 28 Mar. 1917, Evening ed.: 1. Print.

111. Ohles, John F., ed. *Biographical Dictionary of American Educators.* Vol. 1. Westport, Connecticut: Greenwood, 1978. Print.

112. Oliver, Paul. *Savannah Syncopators: African Retentions in the Blues.* New York: Stein and Day, 1970. Print.

113. Olmsted, Denison. *Memoir of Eli Whitney, Esq.* New Haven: Durrie & Peck, 1846. Print.

114. "Original Stardust Enterprises." *Original Stardust - Hollywood Memorabilia.* N.p., n.d. Web. 23 Sept. 2009. <http://www.hollywoodwalkoffamestardust.com/catalog/product_info.php?cPath=26&products_id=32>.

115. Pearson, Barry Lee. *"Sounds so good to me" the bluesman's story.* Philadelphia: Pennsylvania UP, 1984. Print.

116. Pennell, P. M. "How to Make a Cigar Box Violin." *Popular Homecraft* Feb.-Mar. 1935: 338-39. Print.

117. Perrin, Noel. "Foreword." Foreword. *The American Boy's Handy Book.* By Daniel Carter Beard. New York: Nonpareil Book: Scribner, 1890. Iii-Xiii. Print.

118. "Potaro Coarse, Coarse Gold." *The Galveston Daily News* 31 May 1896: 14. Print.

119. "Prima Donna is Vodvil Feature." *The La Crosse Tribune* 20 Nov. 1912: 4. Print.

120. "THE REBEC PAGE." *Rutgers University - Camden Campus.* Web. 10 Dec. 2007. <http://crab.rutgers.edu/~pbutler/rebec.html>.

121. Richards, John. "A Cigar-Box Banjo." *Harper's Young People: An Illustrated Weekly* VII.330 (1886): 262-63. Print.

122. Richards, John. "A Cigar-Box Banjo." *Iowa State Reporter* [Waterloo] 25 Mar. 1886: n. pag. Print.

123. Ridgefield Archives Committee. *Images of America: Ridgefield*. Portsmouth: Arcadia: Tempus, 1999. Print.

124. Roberts, Ronald. *Making a Simple Violin and Viola*. New York: David & Charles PLC, 1975. Print.

125. Ross, Steve. *Prof. Hammerfinger's Indestructible Toys*. New York: Oliver: Charles Scriber's Sons, 1975. Print.

126. "Roy Clark - Product 32." *Hollywoodwalkoffamestardust.com*. 10 Feb. 2007. Web. <http://www.hollywoodwalkoffamestardust.com/catalog/product_info.php?cPath=26&products_id=32>.

127. Russell, Tony. *Blacks Whites and Blues*. Ed. Paul Oliver. New York: Stein and Day, 1970. Print.

128. "Sabbath School Workers Coming." *The Daily Courier* [Connellsville, PA] 11 May 1917, Evening ed.: 1. Print.

129. San, Ohta, and Jan Friedson. *Ukulele O Hawaii: Instructions for Beginning & Advanced Students of the Ukulele*. Honolulu: Kamaka Hawaii, 1973. Print.

130. Samuels, S. H. "A Homemade Hawaiian Ukulele." *Popular Mechanics* Jun. 1917: 946. Print.

131. "Satis N. Coleman." *Untitled Document*. N.p., n.d. Web. 21 Sept. 2009. <http://www.sandyn.com/women/coleman.htm>.

132. Scarry, Richard. *Richard Scarry's Best Stories Ever.* New York: Golden, 1971. Print.

133. Schulz, Charles M. *The Complete Peanuts 1950-1952.* Seattle: Fantagraphics Books, 2004. Print.

134. Schulz, Charles M. *The Complete Peanuts 1953-1954.* New York: Fantagraphics Books, 2004. Print.

135. Scult, Mel, ed. Communings of the Spirit: The Journals of Mordecai M. Kaplan, 1913-1934. Detroit: Wayne State UP, 2001. Print.

136. Shapiro, Nat, and Nat Hentoff. *Hear Me Talkin' To Ya: The Story of Jazz as Told By the Men Who Made It.* Toronto: General Company, 1966. Print.

137. "Short wavers Get Japanese Rhythm." *Oakland Tribune* 3 May 1935, sec. D: 40. Print.

138. Sitsky, Larry. *Music of the Twentieth-century Avant-garde: A Biocritical Sourcebook.* Westport, Conn: Greenwood, 2002. Print.

139. Smith, George. "Willie Weakbean Writes a Letter to the Editor." *Syracuse Herald* 10 Oct. 1926: n. pag. Print.

140. Spaeth, Sigmund. *A History of Popular Music in America.* New York: Random House, 1948. Print.

141. Spicer, H. "Walks Up Hill." Ed. William Harrison Ainsworth. *The New Monthly Magazine* 1853: 292-97. Print.

142. "Splendid Bill at Majestic Theatre." *The La Crosse Tribune* 2 Jan. 1914: 8. Print.

143. ""Stale Bread" Lacoume - Traces Jazz Back to '90s." *The Daily Courier* [Connellsville, PA] 6 Mar. 1936: 15. Print.

144. Strasser, Susan. *Waste and Want A Social History of Trash.* New York: Owl Books, 2000. Print.

145. "Summer in Spain Inspires City Guitarist to Resume Composing." *Albuquerque Journal* 22 Sept. 1968, sec. B: 11. Print.

146. "SUNDAY YOU WILL HEAR?." *Winnipeg Free Press* 19 Jan. 1935: n. pag. Print.

147. Sutherland, W. J. "Cigar Box Violin." *Science and Mechanics* Feb.-Mar. 1948: 109-12. Print.

148. "TALENTED RUSSIANS FEATURE OFFERING AT GRAND OPERA HOUSE." *The Galveston Daily News* 20 Feb. 1924: n. pag. Print.

149. Tangerman, E. J. *Whittling and Woodcarving.* New York: Dover Publications, Inc., 1936. Print.

150. "TENNESSEE ?FIDDLER? ELECTED TO CONGRESS." *Jefferson City Post-Tribune* 5 Aug. 1938: 3. Print.

151. "Thrifty Youth Is Manufacturer Of His Own Guitar." *La Crosse Tribune And Leader-Press* 25 May 1945, morning ed.: 10. Print.

152. "Try It A Cigar Box Strumming Guitar." *Oakland Tribune* 9 May 1954: n. pag. Print.

153. Twain, Mark. *Autobiography of Mark Twain.* Ed. Charles Neider. New York: Perennial Classics: Harper Collins, 2000. Print.

154. "Ukulele." *The Modesto Evening News* 2 Aug. 1922: n. pag. Print.

155. ""Uncle Ned" Tells of Reception Of Mrs. Patrick Campbell." *The Davenport Daily Leader* 19 Jan. 1902: n. pag. Print.

156. "Unusual Music Instruments Are Played by Evangelist." *The Progress* [Clearfield, PA] 20 Oct. 1949: 20. Print.

157. Van Abburgh, J. C. "PUBLIC SCHOOL ORCHESTRA." *The Daily Inter Lake* [Kalispell, Montana] 22 Oct. 1922: 4. Print.

158. "Vaudeville Attraction at Grand Saturday and Sunday." *Stevens Point Daily Journal* 15 June 1914: 1. Print.

159. *Vaudeville*. Prod. Rosemary Garner, Tamar Hacker, and Gary Gibson. American Masters, 1997. DVD.

160. "Violins From Scrapwood." *Popular Science* Nov. 1940: 110-11. Print.

161. "Violins." *The Newark Daily Advocate* 20 Nov. 1914: 7. Print.

162. Vlach, John M. *The Afro-American Tradition in Decorative Arts*. Athens: Brown Thrasher Books: Georgia UP, 1990. Print.

163. Volk, Terese M. *Music, Education, and Multiculturalism Foundations and Principles*. New York: Oxford UP, USA, 2004. Print.

164. Vroom, Frank W. "How to Make a Jazzolin from a Broomstick." *Popular Science* July 1920: 110-11. Print.

165. Wardlow, and Komara. *Chasin' That Devil Music: Searching for the Blues.* San Francisco: Miller Freeman Books, 1998. Print.

166. Warford, John. "Out of the Usual Order." *The Perry Pilot* 1883. Print.

167. Whiteman, Paul. "On Broadway With Walter Minchell." *The Brownsville (Texas) Herald* 24 July 1935: 5. Print.

168. Wigginton, Eliot, ed. *Foxfire 3.* New York: Anchor Books: Doubleday, 1975. Print.

169. "Youans Wins Prize for Being Best C. C. Fiddler." *Mason City Globe-Gazette* 29 Dec. 1927: n. pag. Print.

CPSIA information can be obtained at www.ICGtesting.com
Printed in the USA
LVOW10s2243020214

372035LV00011B/115/P